SOMEONE TO TALK TO

FINDING PEACE, PURPOSE, AND JOY AFTER TRAGEDY AND LOSS; A RECIPE FOR HEALING FROM TRAUMA AND GRIEF

SAMANTHA M. WHITE

Yankee Drummer Press, Framingham, Massachusetts

Yankee Drummer Press
40 Speen Street, Suite 106
Framingham, Massachusetts 01701-1898
www.yankeedrummerpress.com

All events related in this book are true to the best of my understanding. Names of some people and places have been changed to protect the privacy of those who requested it or are protected by law and the Code of Ethics of the profession of social work. The clinical case in Chapter 24 is a blending of several actual representative cases, with all names and identifying details changed.

Portions of Chapters 29 and 30 first appeared in the anthology *I'm Here, and Other Memoirs from the Wellness Community of Greater Boston*, Peggy Rambach, editor, ©2007
Portions of Chapter 19 appeared in a different form as an article in *Daily Word*, March/April, © 2011 Unity®.

Printed in the United States of America

ISBN 978-0-9832142-0-5

Cover photograph ©Jo Ann Tomaselli / Dreamstime.com
Author photograph ©Jim Spirakis / jspd.com

Dedicated with abiding love and gratitude
to my wonderful husband,
Dave,
who makes me possible,

and to my elder daughter,
light and pride of my life,

and to the blessed memory of
my younger daughter,
gentle angel,
and my parents,
Irene and Nathan Sokoletsky.

Our love is eternal.

Acknowledgments

My humble thanks to Mother Miriam Pollard, who has always encouraged me, and to Rabbi Elias Lieberman, who saw me through much of what is written here. You have been my great spiritual teachers. My thanks also to Marilyn and John Darack, Sandra Orenstein, and Robert Tuck for walking the way with me and believing in me. Thank you Ruth Fishel and Nancy Wainer for your strong support and encouragement for writing this book. Thank you to my readers MarySusan Douglass, Janet Drake, Carole Eilenberg, and Pam Teibel for your invaluable assistance in bringing this book to completion, and to Cecile Kaufman for your skillful and sensitive copyediting. And effusive thanks, of course, to my editor *extraordinaire*, Margo Melnicove, for not holding back from telling me what I needed to do to make this a better book than I ever could have written without your keen sense of story and your "ear" for the written word.

Dave, my husband, my gift, my ally, thank you for tolerating my long hours at my desk, for being my read-aloud audience, and for your gracious willingness to share our life with this project for the many months it has consumed.

Many more people helped, in many ways. I regret I cannot list you all. Writing this book has long been my ambition and my life's work, but it never would have become a reality without the strong support of all of you. I am deeply and forever grateful.

CONTENTS

An Open Letter To A Friend Suffering From Loss

My Dear Friend,

"How do you live with what happened?" you asked me.

The answer is both simple and complex—simple in that what worked for me can be stated in only five steps, complex in that the steps were not necessarily sequential. I moved back and forth among them, sometimes focusing on one and at other times using them all simultaneously, and it took much longer than I wished.

So it was simple, although not quick, and it was complex, but never overwhelming. The most important thing I can tell you is that healing and knowing joy again are possible.

Many times during the hard work and long months of writing this book, in mental and physical pain from reliving the trauma I'd been through, I wanted to abandon the project altogether and get on with my joyful life. Each time, you urged me to keep writing, for you and others like you who may benefit from knowing how I achieved healing that went beyond recovery, to growth.

"I need to know," you said, "how you get up every morning and enter the day eagerly, joyfully, with all the pain that must be in your heart."

Although our losses are not identical, people who suffer face many of the same challenges. The following chapters recount my own transformational journey. They contain intimate descriptions of significant events in my life, told with full candor, because I wanted you to know how the recipe for healing from trauma and grief, presented in the book's final pages, emerged from my own personal experiences.

Now that I have written my book, I am grateful to you for encouraging me to stay with it. I hope it helps you find your way out of the painful place you are in. I made the long climb out of darkness and heartache to achieve peace, purpose, and unexpected joy. I believe you can, too.

Know that I care deeply about you and support your healing and growth.

Fondly,

Samantha

Part I

Falling

One

MAY 1988

The pounding of the heavy brass knocker against the front door woke me from a fitful sleep. The alarm clock glowing green in the darkness read 3:15 a.m., not a good omen. In bare feet and a pink cotton granny nightgown—that I would later stuff into a wastebasket and never wear again—I padded down the carpeted stairs, needing only the moonlight pouring through the windows to show me the way. I flipped on the lamp in the living room and the switch for the outside light, peered through the glass pane in the door, and found myself face-to-face with my ex-husband, Paul. The pane of glass between us notwithstanding, this was the closest we had been to each other in the more than three years since we had separated.

Some part of my brain registered the enormous unlikelihood of this visit, and therefore its frightening significance. Something terrible was about to happen, and I had to stop it. As I unlocked the door and invited him in, I felt myself evaporate and drift out of my body. The part of me that remained standing at the door pretended this was something else, an afternoon visit, he just happened to stop by—even though he had never been to my house (although he lived nearby), hadn't called or spoken to me in years, and had never made eye contact or nodded or said hello when we had seen each other at the Unitarian-Universalist church to which we both still belonged—and yet here he was, and it was easier for me to pretend we were good friends keeping a tea date than it was to let in any reality of why he might be here. In my denial I escaped into what was easy and familiar. The dead of night suddenly became the middle of the afternoon.

"Please sit down," I said warmly to the man who had announced he wanted a divorce after twenty-five years of marriage. "Would you like some tea?"

"No," he said, heading for the couch.

I floated above the fireplace and looked down at us, watching myself as I sat primly on the rocking chair facing him, folded my hands in my lap, and waited for him to tell me why he had stopped by. I saw myself smile as I waited, curious but not alarmed, because I had shut off all my inner alarms the moment I had seen his face through the windowpane in the door.

He stared straight ahead, beyond me, at a vague point somewhere in the middle of the room. "Becca . . . " he said, and stopped. Becca was our younger daughter, Rebecca. He began again. "Becca . . . has been in a fatal car crash."

Fatal! Who died? I was about to ask, when he lowered his head into his hands, hiding his face, and his shoulders heaved with silent, wracking sobs.

I gasped in sudden understanding. It was Becca who had died! But I had talked with her on the phone only a few hours earlier! She was only twenty! How could she be dead?

My first instinct, as it had always been with him, was to comfort him, and as my floating self watched from the ceiling, my pink-clad self rushed to the couch and sat beside him. I saw myself wrap my arms around him and put my head next to his, and heard myself make crying sounds. My tears weren't real, nothing was real, what he was telling me couldn't be real, but I had heard him speak, watched him crumple, and somehow I felt obligated to comfort him, to hold him, to draw close, to behave like a good woman, a caring ex-wife. I also wanted to be held, because I knew he had just told me something terrible, something I had heard all my life was the worst thing that could happen to a person, to lose a child.

But he didn't move, only sat there, rigid, staring at that spot in front of him, swallowed, and went on with his report. I pulled back a little but stayed beside him, and listened.

The police had come to his door a half hour earlier with the news, and he had taken on the awful task of telling me. He gave me a few details—where it had happened, who she had been with, and that two of her friends had died, too.

I felt nothing. I acted calm. This could not be happening to me, because everyone said it was absolutely the worst thing that could happen, and I lived an ordinary life, exceptional things didn't happen to me, but here he was, telling me that our daughter had been in a fatal car crash. He couldn't even say she'd been killed, that she was dead, it was too much for him to accept, too.

4

The police had told him we should call the state trooper barracks, and had given him a telephone number and a name. An officer told us what happened. Becca had been a passenger in a car with friends. The car had left the road. Her body had been thrown. The police had identified her from her driver's license in her purse. The officer expressed his condolences.

"Thank you very much," I said as we hung up.

"Now what do we do?" Paul and I asked each other.

Tell someone, we agreed.

I called my brother, Dennis. "I'm sorry to wake you," I said, still polite, "but something terrible has happened."

"What? he asked.

"*Really* terrible," I said. "It's . . . Becca," I said, and started to cry, this time for real. "She was in a fatal car crash."

"Is she dead?" he asked, and I tried to say yes, but the word got caught in my throat and came out as a squawk.

"What can I do to help you?" he asked.

"Please tell Mother and Dad," I said. I knew too well the form their pain always took—protesting, resisting, arguing, frantically needing to be assured it wasn't true.

"I will," he promised.

While Paul called his sister, I grabbed something to wear without thinking about what I chose. I couldn't think. I was numb, which felt better than the anguish I was avoiding. Numb was good. Businesslike. I was good at being businesslike.

Then we went to tell Sasha, just turned twenty-two, that her only sister had died, phoning her first to tell her we were on our way. She was waiting for us on the sidewalk in front of her apartment, and told us afterward that she knew something terrible had happened and who it had happened to, when she saw us together in Paul's car coming the wrong way down her one-way street.

Back at my house the three of us sat at the kitchen table, trying to figure out what to do next. I wanted to huddle close, hold hands, hug. Sasha had hugged me and then her father when we'd met at the curb, but then we had all detached, and now she told me she wanted to be taken to her friend's house.

My heart went cold and I said, "Not here? Won't you stay here?"

"No," she said, sadly but firmly, "I really need to go to Barb's house."

Paul said, "I need to go home," and he rose from the table and quickly left.

I drove Sasha to Barb's house and watched her go in, to where her friend and her friend's mom would comfort her. I ached, feeling robbed of my rightful role as her mother. I wanted to be the mother to comfort her. And I needed her to be with me.

I thought back to when the family living across the street from us had lost their son, and everyone had said, "What a wonderful family!" as we watched them draw tight, Dad and Mom and the kids, saw how they clustered around the door as they received callers, thanked people for coming, for bringing food, and later huddled in the driveway, dressed in black, awaiting the limousine bound for the cemetery, and that after they came back to the house, the grown children stayed for a long time. "Such a fine family," everyone had agreed.

All I had ever really wanted in my life was a family, and I had had my family, a wonderful family. We had been so happy, and so close! We had skied, sailed, camped, and hiked together, cooked and taken our meals together, shared our lives with each other. People had looked to us as a model of how happy marriage and family life could be, seen our obvious joy as proof that marriage could be great, despite anything they had heard or been through themselves. But that was before things changed and our family dissolved.

I wished we could have stayed together that day and given comfort to each other, as we would have in the days when our family was intact, but too much had happened to us to ever behave like a family again. Even now, when we shared a common tragedy and needed love most, all we could do was turn away from each other and seek comfort alone, or from friends.

I drove back home.

Paul picked me up later in the morning to meet with the minister at the church and to go to the funeral home, the cemetery, the florist. I was a woman with a job to do, and as with all jobs, I did it, and I did it right. Funeral service, pine casket, burial plot, yellow roses, all checked off. We stopped for coffee and then Paul took me back to my cottage and I was alone again.

Alone.

I had never felt the loss of my family as much as I did that day. I didn't know what to do. Sit? Walk? Stand? I couldn't think of anything I could do, was supposed to do.

I wanted to call Nick, my fiancé, but I couldn't do that because he had told me just a few days ago that he was not my fiancé, that his marriage proposals had been a sham, that he had been lying to me for two years, and now he was away with another woman whom he had known far longer than me. I was not to call him while he was with her.

I dreaded the prospect of going to bed alone, touching no one from the time I lay down until morning, maybe longer. I craved touch.

I called my friends Marilyn and Mike, and left a message on their voicemail. "Hi, this is Sam. My daughter Becca was killed last night and I think I'm going to need some help but I don't know what ki . . ." and here my throat closed, my voice broke, I couldn't even finish the word. I hung up.

I tried to visualize Becca, to lock onto an image of what she looked like, how her voice sounded, and found that I couldn't. I tried, but all I could remember was the first time I saw her, tiny, with lots of dark hair, eyes that barely opened, and a little rosebud mouth. We had expected our little girl in March, Sasha's birthday month, too. But Rebecca had been born in February, a preemie, weighing only five pounds. I'd held my new baby to my chest and rocked her, spoke to her, sang to her, as I had to Sasha when she was an infant. For the rest of my life I would remember Rebecca just this way. My baby.

When I had placed the blanket-wrapped bundle of baby in Sasha's outstretched arms, my own beneath hers for support, I said, "This is your baby sister Rebecca!"

Sasha's eyes had glowed, as had Paul's and mine, and she said very softly, "Hi, Becca."

And so Rebecca had her nickname.

My heart had overflowed with joy at my wonderful family—my husband, my big-girl toddler, and my baby.

My mother and I had chosen Rebecca's coming-home outfit together, a gown that was printed with tiny purple violets and tied at the bottom, and a pale yellow fleece jacket with tiny mitten sleeves and matching cap and bunting, to protect her from the cold New England weather. When we dressed her to leave the hospital, she was almost buried in all the layers of soft cotton—the white undershirt, the gown—and thick fleece. I sang to her all the way home.

Paul and I had placed a straw bassinet with a pink liner on the floor beside our bed, and when her *Zaide*, Paul's father, came to meet his newest grandchild and asked where she was, we pointed to the basket on the floor where she lay sleeping on the quilted, white mattress pad, almost hidden in a cocoon of pink and white flannel receiving blankets, looking like a tiny pile of laundry.

I couldn't remember anything else about her. Only that she was my baby.

I sat. I walked from room to room. I felt shell-shocked, stunned, confused. *What had happened? What was going to happen now?* The question that burned at me most was, *what am I supposed to do?* I had always known what I was supposed to do, but I had no idea what I was supposed to do now. What did other people do when this happened to them?

I called my friend Steve at his office, told him what had happened, and asked him to call a few friends and ask them to spread the word. Maybe they would know what I was supposed to do and they would tell me.

"Where are you now?" Steve asked.

"At home," I said.

"Who is with you?"

"No one," I said.

"You mean you're alone?"

"Yes."

"I think I should come over," he said.

I didn't know why. "I'm fine," I said, believing it.

But Steve showed up at my door an hour later, right behind my cousin Mark, who had learned about Becca's death from the morning television newscasts.

I asked Mark why he had come. "You hardly knew Becca," I said, truly surprised he had come all this way, found my house, and showed up in the middle of the afternoon on a workday.

"But I've always felt close to you," he said.

"Yes," I said, agreeing that I felt close to him, too. But why was he here? I was drifting away again from what was real, had happened, was happening now. This was less real than a fairy tale, it was totally unimaginable, and I still couldn't take it in.

8

Friends arrived throughout the day and evening. I behaved graciously, hospitably, but they knew I was dazed and understood what lay beneath my behavior better than I did.

When Marilyn came through the front door and saw me, she opened her arms, and cried "Oh, Sam!" She embraced me and wept, and I wondered why. Why was she crying? Had something bad happened to her? Was she going to tell me what it was?

The hands of friends peeled us apart, and someone took Marilyn into the kitchen as Steve led me away.

"Why is Marilyn crying?" I asked him.

When he didn't answer, I ventured, "Do you think it's because of Becca?" Marilyn hadn't been very close to Becca, I thought, why would she be so distraught?

"Yes," he said, "I think it's because of Becca."

"Oh," I said, puzzled. I didn't understand why others would be upset, but I was so grateful they were all here because I needed people to tell me what to do. I couldn't think about anything—food, sleep, anything. The thinking part of my brain had shut down.

My feelings had shut down, too. I knew something terrible had happened, but I couldn't let whatever it was reach me because it would hurt me more than I could bear. So I held myself together. Tightly. Cold and hard like steel.

The only emotions available to me were my terror of feeling anything and a strange sadness, strange because it did not stem from Becca's death, that was impossible, she could not have died, but from the inability of Paul and Sasha and me to function together as a family, holding each other up. And from the fact that Nick, in whose arms I had felt love and safety, was gone.

I was emotionally depleted, in a very deep, dark hole, already worn to shreds by all that had happened before—the loss of my marriage despite my five-year struggle to save it, the disintegration of my family, Nick's betrayal—and I couldn't let myself see where I was because the depth and darkness of the hole I was in threatened to make me instantly, totally insane.

So, without knowing how or why, I turned to stone, unseeing, unknowing, unfeeling, except for the guilt that gnawed silently at the edge of my awareness. I had made a difficult choice eight years earlier, to honor what I thought were my husband's needs (but were perhaps really my own) over my daughters', and maybe I had stayed in the marriage too long. Those were the years—from 1980 to 1985—that Becca had started hanging around with kids who were

9

trouble. Maybe if I had left Paul and taken her away sooner, she would be alive now.

I would spend years asking myself what I should have done differently, why I had stayed so long, why I hadn't been able to help him, help us, help her, maybe save her.

Two

Eight years earlier, news of the first disaster had also arrived with Paul through the front door, but in the guise of a normal glitch in our family life. It came softly on a sunny day to a different house, the house that later, in the divorce proceedings, would be referred to as "the marital home."

I was upstairs, making the beds on a June morning in 1980. My first thought when I heard the screen door downstairs wheeze open and slowly sigh shut was, What's wrong? The clock on the bookcase headboard read 10:20, too early for anyone else to be home. I heard the latch click sharply as it caught, but no one called up the stairs. I turned away from fluffing pillows and smoothing blankets, and stepped out into the hallway.

Paul stood in the small patch of sunlight on the flagstone tiles in the foyer, holding his leather briefcase and looking up at me. His face was unusually pale. I thought he might be ill.

"I've been fired," he said softly, choking slightly on the words, disbelief in his voice.

I walked down the stairs and stopped at the bottom step, where our heights matched, and slid my arms around him, and held him. He was almost fifty, in a new career as a marketing account manager. We had been married twenty years, and I was still in love with him. I knew the blow to his confidence and self-esteem hurt much more than the loss of work and income.

In the kitchen, over coffee, he told me about the boss's speech ("Hate to lose you, but revenues are down."), the emptying of his desk, the saying of good-byes. His body slumped as his mood sank. Paul had a history of brief episodes of depression, which I considered normal. I figured everyone loses heart and hope when life becomes difficult, and springs back when things improve. My own moods cycled, too, but we had always managed to be at opposite ends of the mood see-saw, so that I could help him up when he was down, and he could help me when I needed a boost. Now, I wracked my brain for a way to hold his spirits up. "C'mon," I said, "change into jeans and sneakers. Let's get out. We can picnic by the lake, and talk about it there."

While we walked through the woods, I noticed the diamonds of sunlight sparkling on the blue water beyond the trees. "You've found new jobs before," I reminded him. "You'll do it again. I'll help you. We'll get by. Maybe we can even enjoy some time off. Look around, can you see the beauty here?" The trees were in full spring leaf, richly green, the sky bright blue.

'No," he said. "I can't see anything except the abyss in front of me."

Abyss!

Deep in my belly I felt a flutter of fear.

——— ——— ———

We used the dining room table as job search headquarters and spent most of the summer revising his resume and sending it to every possible lead. I had already given up the piano tuning business I had run from home, so I took a job as a secretary at the local hospital to bring in a little money.

Paul's depression alternated with anxiety, so that when he wasn't brooding, he paced. For the first time since I'd known him, he began talking about wanting to die. I pointed out how good our life was, reminding him that we had two beautiful, healthy daughters—Sasha, fourteen, and twelve-year-old Becca, a comfortable home, and a little money in the bank. I urged him to talk to a counselor, but he said he didn't need to. I wanted to call his doctor, tell our families, pull in help for all of us to weather his depression, but he didn't want me to, and I felt a wifely duty to protect his privacy. He spent his empty hours behind the newspaper, reading the want ads, or staring at the television or into space, depressed. His dark mood pervaded the house.

By August, thankfully, responses to our mailings started to dribble in, and Paul had several job interviews. By the end of the month he had a job offer, jumped at it, and went back to work.

We could finally relax, joke and laugh, and be a happy family again.

——— ——— ———

One year later, in 1981, Paul arrived home from work before noon again and grimly announced, "They fired two of us."

I swung into "don't-worry-we'll-lick-this" mode, but inside I began to feel anxious. I dreaded going through another summer like the one before.

Paul's depression was worse than the previous year, and his talk of dying more frequent. He had a plan, and told me how, when he couldn't stand it anymore, he would commit suicide using pills. Being the only person he would confide in was becoming too much for me. He finally agreed that he could use professional help, and asked his primary care doctor for a referral to a psychiatrist.

He came home from his first appointment with a prescription for a new antidepressant medication and an appointment to return in a few weeks. He told me the doctor had said nothing about psychotherapy. I was dubious, but Paul was relieved just to start taking the pills.

Nothing changed, except that we were losing our ability to communicate. I seemed always to have too much to say for Paul to hear, and he too little to say to satisfy my need to understand. Eventually I felt desperate enough to tell a few people, even though I knew Paul would feel humiliated if he knew.

"Paul is depressed," I told my mother.

"Well," she said, "of course he would be. When he finds a new job, he'll be fine."

When my sister-in-law said the same thing, I said, "I'm not talking about just feeling blue. He's clinically depressed." I didn't say "suicidal," still feeling obligated to protect Paul's privacy as much as I could.

"Is he taking medication?" she asked.

"Yes," I said, thinking that would speak to the seriousness of his problem.

"That's good," she said. "That should help him."

I hoped it would. We waited for the medication to kick in and make a difference, but I saw no change.

Why didn't I call a family conference, tell everyone in his family and mine that I was afraid of coming home to find him dead, that he talked about killing himself all the time, and that we needed help?

I had never been good at asking for help, had never learned how. But what I had learned, all too well, was shame. Paul and I had both been raised to understand that certain things were too humiliating to talk about, and mental illness was one of them. So I helped Paul hide the severity of his depression, because in 1981 mental illness carried a heavy stigma, and I had been taught that the obligation of a wife was to make her husband look good, even to his family.

Paul's job hunt eventually paid off. He went back to work late in the summer of 1982, and a sort of normalcy returned. Before dinner each evening he regaled me with excited reports of how much responsibility he was juggling and enjoying.

As time wore on, he began to grumble about the unreasonable volume of work. By winter, his daily reports were about people being laid off. I melted into mild terror as he paced the floor, complaining about his mounting duties and pressing deadlines. The girls kept their distance. He was brimming with agitation and irritability, riding an emotional roller coaster. I wanted to restore his calm and our once happy family, but I felt powerless, and had also become afraid of him. I did not understand how the sweet, mild-mannered man I had fallen in love with had become hostile and belligerent and was now someone I feared, even though I still loved him.

When that job ended, too, his mood crashed. He pushed through another depression and eventually found consulting work to do from home. His mood soared again. But about a year later that work dried up and he hit rock bottom. The medication he had been taking for over two years had not helped at all. He still talked of suicide. I was trying to hold him up, hold all of us up, but my emotions were so tied to his that every job loss, every suicide threat, every angry outburst from him felt like a punch to my gut from which I had to recover before the next one hit, and I was losing ground.

We weren't making ends meet on my salary as a medical secretary, and my skills from the work I had done before becoming a stay-at-home mom were now obsolete. Our savings had run out, and unopened bills with "Final Notice" printed in red on the envelopes were piling up on the desk. Neither of us could bear to look at the stack. One day our electricity was shut off for non-payment. I was wild with worry, imagining us without a roof over our heads, living on the street.

Not knowing how much longer Paul would be unemployed, I needed a way to double my income as soon as possible. He was all in favor of my enrolling in a computer science program at a community college, so I borrowed money from my parents and went back to school.

Months later, when I was well into the program, he said, "I figured out why you're going to school. You're getting ready to leave me."

I was flabbergasted. "I have no intention of leaving you," I protested. "I'm trying to increase my earning power for us, because we need it."

"I don't believe you!" he insisted. "You're going to leave me!" He turned and left the room and I followed him, from the kitchen through the dining room and into the living room—talking to his receding back, as I often found myself doing, trying to penetrate what felt to me like his inability to hear me or to understand anything I said. I felt increasingly isolated and helpless, and always close to tears.

Years later, I would learn that one of the lesser-reported side effects of his medication was paranoia.

———

In May 1983 I completed the computer science program and went to work as an office temp until I found a full-time job using my new skills. I had achieved my goal of doubling my salary. Although Paul had been sure I would leave him, I didn't even consider it.

Now we could pay the bills, but life did not feel significantly easier. Living with Paul's depression and the girls' typically stormy adolescence while working full-time at my new job and also standing guard over Paul in case he tried to follow through on his continuing threats to kill himself could have made anyone tense, fearful, overwhelmed, and exhausted, all of which I was. I couldn't figure out whose fault it was. We were all doing the best we could.

I only knew something needed to change.

Three

Sasha turned sixteen and, with the financial support of my parents, left home to attend a boarding school in New Hampshire. Although I knew it was a good move for her, I cried for weeks, missing her and feeling robbed. I had always thought I'd have her with me until she was eighteen.

Becca stayed close but started hanging around with boys who drank and carried knives, behaved secretively, and avoided making eye-contact with me. I was concerned. She wore a look of pain in her eyes that broke my heart.

One day at work I received a call from the local police.

"Your daughter was skipping school and we just picked her up," the officer said, not unkindly. "The kids she was with are trouble and headed for more trouble. Your daughter is a nice girl, and she shouldn't be with those boys. I'm a father, and I wouldn't want my daughter to have them for friends, and I'm sure you don't, either."

I thanked him and hung up. *What was I supposed to do?* I wondered. *How could I control what she did when she was out of my sight?* I knew she had been skipping school, but she had promised me that would stop. I had dropped her off at school myself that morning, and watched as she turned to wave good-bye and then entered the building. How could I enforce her promises from my office at work? Her father was at home, immobilized by depression. I needed Paul to partner with me, but he couldn't. He was completely debilitated by his symptoms.

I told him that night that I thought he should be doing more, seeking a higher level of treatment, getting better.

"I'm doing the best I can. Just give me time," he pleaded. "When the depression is gone I'll be able to do more, and to look for work. I can't hurry it up. You're my wife. You're supposed to stand by me for as long as it takes. 'In sickness and in health,' remember?"

I wanted to believe him, but I was losing faith in the "just give it more time" approach. Things were getting worse, not better, and I desperately wanted someone to do something about it.

I did some research and found another psychiatrist, someone who came well-recommended and provided psychotherapy in addition to medication, and Paul agreed to meet with him. The new doctor did not accept our insurance, so I turned to Paul's family and asked for money to pay for the new psychiatrist.

"He doesn't need therapy," his mother said. "He needs a job!"

"I agree, Ma," I said. "But without therapy, he's unable to look for one."

A week later a check arrived from his mother, but Paul had changed his mind. "I don't want to switch doctors," he said. "I don't trust anybody else." He cashed the check before I came home from work and opened a personal bank account, preparing for the time he believed I would leave him.

Poor Paul. I had waited too long. The pills that were supposed to treat his illness seemed to have made him more ill, and my options for helping him had run out. I felt like he was drowning, and I was trying to save him, but he was fighting me, and pulling us all down with him. I was desperate and ready to grasp at straws.

———————

I met a woman who told me that at a low point in her life she had changed her name to Victoria and had felt empowered by that. I reasoned that if it had worked for her, maybe it would work for me, too.

And so I decided to take a new name.

My parents had given me the name of a popular child movie star. I was their first baby and, until my brother Dennis was born almost five years later, their little doll. They showered love and attention on me, molding me to be like my on-screen namesake—adorable, polite, precocious, and obedient. As I grew into adolescence and was naturally less obedient, we wrangled, as all teens and parents do. Whenever they reprimanded me, using my name, I felt locked in the identity of a perfect little girl who was never supposed to change, grow up, and become myself.

When I married and swapped my father's last name for my husband's, I still felt trapped in the role of a child. Now I needed to feel my power as an adult, no longer a docile, dependent little girl.

Sam was a nickname I had picked up, somehow, among close friends. Mail for me occasionally arrived addressed to "Samantha," somebody's wrong guess about the reason for my nickname. I looked up the origin and meaning of Samantha. I held my breath, stunned by its aptness, as I read that it is from the Hebrew language, and it means "the woman who listens," or, alternatively, "she is heard." That was who I wanted to be! A woman with the patience and strength to listen with compassion, and to be heard.

Family and friends gathered around us one Sunday afternoon as my friend who is a minister officiated at a ceremony in front of our living room fireplace. My parents were there, mildly bewildered but totally supportive. My mother brought me a pretty lavender turtleneck shirt with my new name embroidered on the neck in white satin stitch, and my aunt brought me a coffee mug with "SAM" printed on the side. The minister explained that naming is traditionally the privilege of whoever takes responsibility for the stewardship of the person being named, and that in naming myself, I was taking responsibility for my own stewardship. The following day, Paul went with me to probate court where the change was made legal, and I began to grow into the feeling, and the meaning, of my new name. I was Samantha, Sam, the woman who listens and is heard. Woman, no longer little girl.

Without fully understanding my own motives, I had taken the first step in assuming control of my life, and remaking myself into a woman who could be happy again.

Four

Friends invited us to their beach cottage on Cape Cod in the summer of 1984. The girls and I went ahead and waited for Paul, who would come along later. I watched out the kitchen window at the spot where he would pull in and park his car. My friend Harriet was at the stove, wearing an apron over her bathing suit, her gray hair damp from steam as she stirred the pot of chowder we would share later at dinner.

"I'm scared," I said, realizing I had begun to shake. I felt my tears rise and spill over.

"Of what?" she asked, laying down the long wooden spoon and coming to stand beside me.

"I never know who is going to step out of that car. Sometimes Paul is all revved up and acting happy, but it's forced, and other times he's in a big, black cloud of depression. He's the only man I've ever loved, and I'm terrified that one day, instead of just talking about suicide all the time, he'll actually kill himself." I put my head in my hands and sobbed. It was the first time I had told anyone about his suicide threats. I felt guilty for betraying him, and was afraid of his reaction for letting his secret out. But I couldn't stand being alone with it any longer.

Harriet had seen what had been happening to us over the past four years, and now she placed her hand lightly on my back. "Sam," she said, "you shouldn't have to suffer this much. It's more than one person can deal with alone. You need help with it, some support. Why don't you see a therapist, someone to talk to who may have some ideas, some solutions, or at least help you carry the weight of it."

I had thought that therapists were for treating the mentally ill, and other than being very unhappy, I considered myself sane and normal. Wouldn't anyone going through the collapse of a marriage that had once been wonderful, seeing her husband's once mild and cheerful personality change so drastically, be sad and hurting? But

Harriet was a sociologist and knew more than I about things like therapy, and she was saying it could help.

This was what I had been needing, someone to give me permission to reach out for professional help, not for Paul, or for us together, but for myself, to deal with my own heartache. I could get *myself* a therapist, because someone I trusted had lovingly told me I deserved to have support.

———————

I carefully shopped for a therapist the way I would for a new winter coat. I needed someone warm and comfortable, who could see me through a lot of tough going, and was affordable. I asked friends for leads, checked the phone book, and made appointments to meet several therapists from various disciplines such as psychology, social work, and psychiatry. I looked for someone both qualified and easy to talk to. I asked the female therapists if they were married, had children, even if they were happy. Some answered readily, others dodged my questions.

Grady, a clinical social worker and the second therapist I interviewed, said, "I'll be happy to tell you, but first I'd like to know why you want to know."

"Because I want to know if it's possible," I said, "to be married with children and happy, or if I'm just chasing a fantasy."

She told me she had been married for twenty-three years, had two daughters, and had never been happier. She was only a little younger than I, attractive and casually dressed in a dark skirt and red sweater, and had a soft and pleasant voice. Something about her felt right, like a cashmere coat slipping lightly over my shoulders. Warm, and a good fit.

But I kept interviewing, because I knew this choice was too important to make hastily. One psychologist took off his shoes and put his feet up on the coffee table between us, possibly an attempt to put me at ease. (It didn't work.) A psychiatric nurse talked with me as we sat in rocking chairs on the front porch of her home. They were both pleasant, but neither felt totally right for me.

One young social worker gave me her solution to my problem in the first ten minutes. "Your husband is not pulling his weight," she said. "You have to leave him. Tell him he has two more weeks to find a job, or he's out. Then you file for divorce."

"But that's not what I want to do," I argued. "I want to save our marriage."

"Then you're not hurting enough," was her astonishing response. "Come back to me when you're in enough pain."

I was speechless. Not hurting enough? Her words rang in my head for weeks afterward. I couldn't imagine how I could be hurting any more.

The psychologists I interviewed had a formal, structured approach, and the nurse and psychiatrist a medical slant that included the use of prescription drugs. The social workers dressed and behaved most informally and were more individual in their styles.

I went back to Grady. Her office was plain, comfortable, and peaceful. I liked her warmth. She agreed to see me for a fee I could afford.

"But I don't want you to tell me I should leave my husband," I said. "I don't want to leave him. I want to help him, and to save our marriage."

"But what if you can't do that?" she asked.

I considered the question. "Then let me come to that conclusion myself," I said. 'Don't tell me what to do. I will have to live with the outcome, so I need to take responsibility for my choices."

"That's fine," she said, and so my therapy began.

Five

Paul's psychiatrist led the way to his office, his wide-shouldered, Harris tweed-covered form almost filling the narrow corridor as I followed him, feeling like a little girl on her way to the principal's office. Inside his cramped workspace, he motioned me into one of the two side-by-side stackable chairs. He squeezed around the big, metal desk and sat in the swivel chair opposite me. The room's only window, behind him, looked onto a brick wall. I was very aware of the empty chair beside me, holding Paul's absence as if it were a living thing. He had given me permission to meet his psychiatrist, but had declined to join me. He seldom left the house anymore.

"I want to know what I can do," I said, "to help my husband get better. What is my role in his recovery?"

"You must get your own needs met," he said. "Paul must understand that he is not the only person in the family with needs."

"But . . . " his answer had surprised me. "What about his needs?"

"His needs are his responsibility," the doctor said, "and your needs are yours. He will get very, very angry at you when you claim your own needs, so angry that he'll probably yell and act as though he wants to . . . to *kill* you! But he won't kill you, he won't even hurt you."

"But who will meet his needs?" I asked.

"He will."

"Can he do that? Take care of himself, find work, be happy, want to live again?" I had assumed more and more of the responsibility for Paul's survival over the years of his illness, until we both had come to believe that I was the only force holding him up.

"Yes, he can do it," the doctor said, and then, with slow emphasis, *"but only if he has to.* Having to do it, and his anger at you for forcing him to do it, will provide him the energy he needs to take care of himself."

I pressed on. "He talks about killing himself. Can I be sure he won't do that?" Keeping him alive seemed to have become part of my exhausting, impossible job.

"Yes," he said with unmistakable and surprising certainty, "you can be sure. He won't kill himself."

I left the building slowly, reeling inwardly, confused and disoriented. I struggled to turn my thinking around from Paul's needs to my own, and was frightened by what I had just been told I must do. I had always been afraid of male anger, had spent my life dodging my father's explosive temper and twenty-four years doing everything I could to avoid igniting Paul's, and now—to help him get well—I was going to have to do the opposite, to deliberately do what I knew would make him angry. I was terrified to do the thing I had always dreaded, to incur the wrath of the man I loved most.

I would have to dig deep inside myself to find the courage to do it, to help him get better, so we could be a happy family again.

I settled into my usual spot at one end of Grady's sofa, my legs curled under me, cradling a mug of tea. She sat in a chair across from me as I told her about my meeting with the psychiatrist. "The problem is," I said, "I think my need is for Paul to return to being my happy and loving husband, and I don't know how to make that happen."

"That's not really about what you need," she said. "You're still talking about him. What if he doesn't want to be happy and loving?"

"But I'm sure he does!" I protested.

"Maybe. But that's still not telling me about your needs. Try it this way—what would make you happy, apart from Paul's happiness?"

I had to think about that a while. "I guess that apart from making Paul happy again, the way he used to be, I have absolutely no idea what my needs are," I said.

"That's what our work here is supposed to help you discover," she said.

And so the goal of my therapy shifted from getting Paul better to finding out what I needed. I finally understood that his choices were out of my control. I had been beating my head against the wall of his unrelenting illness and his need to be free of my badgering him to get more help, accomplishing nothing, while neglecting my children's needs, the quality of my work, and my health. I was emotionally drained.

I was the one who wanted things to change, but all I could change was myself.

Grady and I met every week, talking about what I had wanted to be and do when I grew up (a wife and mother, a writer, healer, teacher, musician), how much of it I had achieved, what I hoped my life might look like in five years, and the direction my life had taken when my marriage changed from ideal to unbearable. I told her about how pain increasingly filled our house.

"Life at home has become so hellish," I told her one day after we had been meeting for a few months, "that I sometimes have a fantasy about just packing up and escaping. It's funny what stops me."

"What?" she asked.

"I don't have any luggage. So in my fantasy I stuff my things into paper grocery sacks, and leave the house juggling paper bags and looking like a homeless person. And then I feel embarrassed, and like a child. When I was five, and my parents told me I was going to the hospital to have my tonsils removed, I packed a grocery bag with toys. My teddy bear stuck out at the top, and the bag tore. I'm afraid that's what will happen again." I paused, imagining myself stumbling along the streets, my clothes falling onto the pavement through the long rips in my brown paper bags. "There's a sale on luggage at the factory store," I mused. "I've been thinking of buying a suitcase, just so I won't feel so trapped."

"I think that's a good idea," she said. "A small price to pay to lose the feeling of being trapped."

My spirits rose as I let go of the pitiful image of myself as a vagrant struggling with overstuffed paper bags.

"You might even think about using it," Grady said.

"How? What do you mean?" I asked.

"You've told me friends have offered you their spare rooms. Would you want to sleep away at a friend's house now and then? Just to see how it feels to get away?"

The year was 1985, five years since the onset of Paul's depression and almost two years since I had begun my computer job. I hadn't taken a break in all that time, and this felt like something I'd like to try.

Paul had no objection.

I bought an overnight bag and began occasionally going to my friends' homes after work, bringing groceries for my supper and breakfast. I left a few changes of clothes in closets that belonged to sons away at college, or daughters living with boyfriends or husbands. I always called Becca, now sixteen, at home with her dad and usually a sleep-over friend from school, for our usual end-of-day review: "How was your day? How are you feeling? What are your plans for tomorrow?" I'd finish with, "I'll see you tomorrow for supper. Sleep well. Call me if you need me. I love you." She knew I would come right home if she needed me. I would have preferred to have her along with me, but she needed to get to school, and I to work, the following morning. She was better off with a friend who would walk to the school bus with her. When I traveled on business, though, I brought her with me, so she could get a break from daily life, see where I worked, and relax and swim in hotel pools, which she loved.

Grady asked, "How does it feel when you sleep away from home?"

I thought about it. "The pain stops," I realized. "My heart doesn't ache when I'm away from him."

"So," she said, "what does that tell you?"

The conclusion was frightening. "That I need to get away from him? But I don't want to leave him!"

"It doesn't mean you have to leave forever," she said. "You could consider taking some respite, a short time away, to rest and think and recharge your batteries. Maybe that's all you need, maybe what Becca needs, too."

I admitted I could use a break from the stress at home.

"How much time do you think you'd need?"

"Three months," I said. My heart lifted at the thought—three months of not coming home to the mess, the gloom, the empty refrigerator, no dinner, and the stranger who used to be my bright, witty, fit, and charming husband, who seemed driven by his depression to eat compulsively, gaining weight, no longer looking like himself, dominating our now joyless house.

After some time apart, I reasoned, maybe we could find the energy to figure out a way to rebuild our crumbling life. Maybe he would find a job. Maybe he would agree to keep house while I worked. Whether or not we could work it out somehow, I needed this break, because I was hurting so much and was so tired, I couldn't even think anymore.

I explained to Paul that I needed a three-month break. I offered to take care of the house, the bills, the girls' needs, if he would prefer to be the one to move out for three months and stay with his family. But he wanted me to be the one to leave.

That evening Becca sat in my favorite little red chintz-covered chair, the one that had been my grandmother's, in the bedroom that was Paul's and mine, and we talked. "Honey," I asked her, "would you be angry if I took you and we moved away from Dad for a little while?"

Looking at me solemnly, she said slowly, "I'd be angry at you if you didn't."

I asked Paul again if he would leave for three months, stay with his mother, his brother, or his cousin, so that Becca wouldn't be uprooted and I could continue paying the household expenses.

"I need to stay here," he said. "If you will be the one to move out, I'll do all I can to help you."

I took that to mean he was on board with the plan, and I agreed to be the one to move out, to make him happy, so he would love me again.

A few days later I told him I had found an apartment close by.

"So you're leaving me," he declared. "I knew you would do this!"

"I'm not leaving you," I insisted. "Leaving is when someone says, 'I'm through here, I'm moving to California, I'm never coming back, and you'll hear from my lawyer.' But I'm moving a few blocks away and telling you it's only for a few months."

He went to the phone and called his mother. "Samantha is leaving me," he told her. "She's divorcing me."

How her heart must have broken to hear that! She loved me, introduced me to her friends as "my daughter," and was ailing, and close to death.

"Ma, I'm not divorcing him," I said loud enough for her to hear as I stood a foot away from him. In my mind's eye I saw him encircled by a thick glass wall, and I was on the outside, banging on it with my fists, kicking, screaming, trying to be heard. But he couldn't hear me.

I knew for sure that I needed the break I was taking.

26

Six

Becca and I packed some clothes and a few things to tide us over, and waited for the movers who would come for her bed, her desk, a table—items we would need during the few months in the apartment. Paul came to where I was lying down, worn out by everything that had led to this point. I wanted to hear him say, "I'm glad you'll get the rest you need and deserve, and I hope it helps you feel happier," but instead he said, "I don't want you to leave."

I heard it as, "I don't want you to get your own needs met, only mine."

I had long ago become too exhausted to try again to explain anything to him.

The movers arrived and Becca and I left.

———————

After we unpacked, we went out for pizza. As we sat in a booth waiting for our food, I said, "I'm sorry, Honey, that it has taken me so long to get you away from how horrible things have been at home. If I had known it was going to go on this long, I would have taken you away sooner." It had been five years.

"A mother is supposed to take care of her children," Becca said softly, "not her husband."

"Well," I said, my thoughts racing ahead so that I could come up with the right words, "it's a very hard call to make. Wives are supposed to stand by and help their husbands, too, and I didn't know who needed me more, or what my responsibility was. So I figured that if I could help Dad get well, that would be for you, too, so you could have your family. If I had known that after all this time he would still not be well, I would have taken better care of you, not him. I need you to forgive me."

"I forgive you," she said, and I grabbed her hands across the table and thanked her.

Becca needed something to lift her spirits. "Name it," I said. "What would you like?"

"Disney World!" she said, her face lighting up. "And Sea World!" She was sixteen and had never been there.

I scrambled to find the best deal, borrowed more money, and took her to Florida for five days. I was in a panic about the possibility of running out of money in Florida, until I came up with a plan. I took the cash we had left after paying for airfare, motel, and tickets to enter the parks, and divided it into envelopes marked with the days of the week. "Each day," I told Becca, "we can spend whatever is in that day's envelope. If there's anything left over, it will go into the next day's envelope, but we can't borrow ahead. On the last day, we can spend whatever is left." That plan gave me peace of mind, and it gave Becca a goal.

It was her first flight, she had a window seat, and she loved it. In Florida, we scrimped by making sandwiches in the motel room and limiting our shopping. On our last day we were able to rent a car, go to Clearwater Beach, and eat at a fancy restaurant. We ended up early in the evening at a store she had spotted on our first day with a huge sign advertising *Jeans! Thousands of Jeans! Jeans!* She tried on jeans for over an hour and bought her two favorites, and then we went back to the motel to relax by the pool once more before flying home the next morning.

I cherish a photo from that trip, now framed on my living room wall, of Becca perched smiling on the edge of the fountain in front of Cinderella's castle, her long blonde hair framing her blue-gray eyes and delicate features, finally looking relaxed and happy again, and like a princess in her garden.

Paul called me at the apartment and told me he wanted a divorce because I had left him. "I'll never be able to trust you not to leave me again," he said.

I was heartbroken. I had never stopped hoping he would understand that I loved him and wanted him to help me save our marriage, and that I just couldn't do it alone. But I guess I had feared all along that if I honored my needs or the children's over his, especially in the state he was in, he would view it as betrayal. We both had been raised to believe that a husband's needs came first, and I still felt guilty.

Becca and I moved back home to try to repair the deep wounds in our family.

———————

Sasha, recently returned from boarding school, was in an automobile accident that demolished her car and left her with several broken bones, lucky to be alive. She needed two extensive surgeries. Now I had a daughter injured and in the hospital, a husband who passed me at home without looking at or speaking to me, a full-time job and a home to manage, and Becca looking frightened and hauntingly sad again. I felt responsible for everyone, and it was more than I could tolerate. I cried to Grady. She listened and helped me to hang on for as long as I could. Paul held fast to his perception that I had abandoned him, and to his decision to divorce. Eventually I saw that my case for saving us—our marriage, our family—was clearly hopeless. We went to court. The judge ordered me to remove Becca from home, take her somewhere else to live, away from the hell our life as a family had become.

Many years later, Paul told me, "I never understood why you came back, that time."

"It was always my plan to come back," I said. "I had told you before we separated that it was temporary."

"I never understood why you came back," he repeated.

From the first faint hint of trouble until the time we could no longer find a way to live together under the same roof had taken five and a half excruciating, damaging years, from which it would take me much longer to recover, because more losses were about to happen that would disrupt my life, and my healing, even further.

Seven

Becca and I moved out again, this time to a rustic little cottage in the woods surrounding a pond. She was still near her friends and had a cozy room of her own at ground level with a spiral staircase connecting it to our living room directly above.

Christmas was only two weeks away. Although Paul and I had been raised in Jewish families and were proud of our heritage, we shared an openness to all spiritual wisdom and traditions, and had passed this on to our daughters. One year, when Hanukkah and Christmas happened to fall at the same time, we had a small Christmas tree in front of the living room window, and a menorah shining on the windowsill in the dining room. Friends told us that from outside, the house looked as though two families lived there—a Christian family on one side and a Jewish one on the other. We enjoyed hearing this, because we wanted to embrace the best parts of everything, and adding light at the darkest time of the year was, for us, an expression of joy. Although I didn't know the word then, I suppose we were universalists, respecting all beliefs, even paganism, agnosticism, and atheism.

Now, in the cottage in the woods, Becca wanted the biggest, most beautiful Christmas tree to be had. We wrestled the largest tree we could find into the cottage by ourselves, hacking off the topmost branch so that it could stand straight. I strung the lights and she added the decorations, and that night we had our first Christmas Eve without Dad and Sasha, just Becca and me, wrapping presents for each other and celebrating being in a lovely, peaceful place, trying to stay on top of the sea of sadness flowing all around us at the ending of the family we had been.

Late that night I sat up in bed and tried to draw, with pastel crayons and colored markers, what my heart held. My drawing showed the scene outside my window—fresh snow blanketing the ground, outlining the barren trees, and weighing down the branches of the evergreens. Bright stars shared the black sky with a huge, perfect white disc of a full moon lighting up the landscape and gleaming off the bright red cap of the new bird-feeder—stocked and ready for the birds to find—hanging on the porch. When I finished the drawing and looked at it, I saw again the beauty of where we had landed and the hope for a future of wishes fulfilled. I labeled the drawing, *Christmas Eve, 1985.*

By taking the break from Paul that I needed, I had closed a door I hadn't meant to, and found myself in a new life that, for the first time in my life, was my own.

I loved waking to the view outside my window—the woods, the snow, and on clear days the sun rising behind the trees, changing the color of the snow from red-orange to pink to yellow to brilliant white. I lay on my pillow and watched the show with gladness and gratitude. The pain I had lived with for so many years—fearing Paul's anger, his threats of suicide, feeling the largeness of his presence and the withdrawal of his love, the worry about expenses my income alone couldn't meet—had, as if by magic, vanished. I watched the winter birds who had found the feeder and came in greater numbers at each dawn—chickadees, tufted titmice, and the brilliantly red cardinals who picked up the fallen seed on the porch.

I also loved coming home from work each day to our sanctuary to find Becca studying, watching TV, or having a visit with a friend. She was seventeen and enjoying our new situation. I came to know her friends better, in that little house, where the mood was light, happy, and safe. She had left school, with my blessing, and was studying for her GED.

She passed the exam, but the policy of the school department was to withhold the diploma until her class graduated. So she went to work at a job that suited her perfectly, as a homemaker for shut-ins. She spent each day at the homes of ill or elderly people who couldn't get about, doing their laundry and shopping and fixing their lunches, and putting her natural skills of gentle caring to good use. Her supervisor called to tell me how much the clients loved having her come. She was sweet, pretty, and kind, and brightened up their days.

I could afford the rent on our charming cabin, although just barely, and Marilyn and Mike, our landlords who lived in another cottage on the pond, were becoming my good friends. I had nothing left to fear or worry about, and I was euphoric.

My friend Steve, divorced longer than I, told me, "Some people feel that high, at first. But it doesn't last, it gives way to the opposite feeling, the crash one would expect when a marriage has failed."

Not me, I thought. *This freedom, this joy, is wonderful and real.*

———————

I practiced my newfound freedom, doing little things I wanted to do without having to get someone else's agreement: playing my own choice of music when I was home alone (Paul had never left the house during the last few years), inviting friends, old and new, to join Becca and me for wine and cheese, or a candlelit supper.

One night when Becca was sleeping at a friend's house, I awoke at about three a.m., not tired anymore. I lay awake in the dark until I realized there was no one with me who would be disturbed, or ask what I was doing, to whom I owed any courtesy or explanation—and I turned on the light. No one said, "Turn it off, I'm trying to sleep." I rose from the bed and went into the living room, turning on all the lights. No one asked, "What are you doing? It's three a.m.!" I was enjoying this and wanted to test it more. I slipped into jeans and a sweatshirt, and no one said, "Where are you going at this hour!"

Exploring this first-time-in-my-life autonomy, I left the house and started up my car to go for a ride before dawn. I had never done this. The freedom was so new, so fresh! Nervous about the possible danger a woman can meet when out alone in the dark, I wondered where I would go. I remembered the drive-through ATM machine at the bank and decided to go there and withdraw twenty dollars without leaving my car.

That worked well and I was ready for something else. I drove to a well-lit, all-night gas station and put twenty dollars worth of gas into my car.

Jubilant at being out on my own, knowing that no one was telling me I was crazy for doing this, and that there was no one to judge me anymore but myself, I realized I had tested my independence and passed the test. I drove home, got undressed, turned out the lights, and went back to sleep, smiling and feeling new. I told Grady all about it the next day, and she congratulated me for expanding my boundaries.

The euphoria continued, surprising and thrilling. I was on top of the world. People at work made comments. "Sam, you seem so happy!"

"My husband and I have separated for good," I'd respond, and their expressions would change to looks of shock or confusion. It was not what I had expected, either, that I would feel so lighthearted and happy.

————————

Real as these feelings may have been, they were also temporary. After a month or so, I started the slide down into another side of my new reality. I began to feel alone, discarded, misunderstood.

The only other time I had been so totally on my own I was twenty-one, fresh out of college, sharing an apartment with roommates, and full of hope and optimism. But now I had been "dumped" by my life partner, making me a reject. I had just turned forty-eight and was afraid of the unknown life that stretched ahead of me.

In therapy, I talked with Grady about my damaged sense of self. "I don't feel worth loving, anymore," I said. "Paul knew me better than anyone. He was the only person who 'got' me, and he stopped loving me. Now I feel worthless and unlovable."

"You relied on him for your self worth," she observed. "You gave him the power to make you worthy or unworthy. That's a lot of power you gave away."

"What do I do now?" I asked.

"You take responsibility for your self worth, build your own sense of value."

"All by myself? How do I do that? Tell myself I'm wonderful?"

"Yes, but you don't need to listen only to yourself, it doesn't have to come from just one person. Make it a mix of your own sense and the sense of people who know you, people whose opinions matter to you."

"Like who?"

"Does my opinion of you matter?" she asked.

"Very much," I said. "Would you tell me what you think of me?"

"Of course," she said. "I think you have spunk, and that's a very positive quality, one that I admire."

"What exactly is spunk?" I wanted to know.

"I'd say it's 'energy from within,'" she said. "You have an energy that lifts you up and has the same effect on others."

I felt pleased, and started to jot that down in a small notebook I carried in my purse.

"If I were you," Grady said, "I'd take that notebook around and ask your good friends, the ones who know you well, what they like about you, and write it all down."

This became a project I continued for a long time. Harriet told me I was brave. Someone else told me I was funny. I remembered some of my accomplishments and added them to the notebook. One day when someone told me I was "very pretty," I grabbed the book and made sure that made its way onto a page. On days when I was feeling low, I'd pull out the book and read nice things about myself that I could believe, because they came from people I trusted.

Slowly, I began to feel worth loving. I also reminded myself that I still had two lovely daughters and my health, my education, my job— and it would have to be enough. As for romantic love, I knew I wanted to venture there eventually, but I wasn't ready to look for it because I couldn't bear to be hurt again.

Eight

My next wedding anniversary loomed as an occasion for mourning the loss of all the hopes and dreams I thought Paul and I had shared. I was afraid of being alone with my sorrow, and needed a way to protect myself and maybe find some peace with my solitary life. Still drawn to Buddhism from my college days, I went to the Insight Meditation Society in Barre, Massachusetts, for my first three-day silent retreat.

There were about a hundred of us in the retreat, which was led by Sharon Salzberg, one of the founders of the society and a renowned Buddhism teacher. She instructed us in the ways of the retreat house and the practice of insight meditation, and then we sat in silence on our mats and blankets spread out on the floor of the meditation hall. I found the silence difficult at first, but quickly came to love the peaceful quiet. We walked in silence, ate in silence, bathed and dressed and worked in silence, for three blissful days.

Sometimes, though, as I sat in silence, I remembered why I had come, what I had wanted to get away from—the remembrance of the loss of my marriage—and found myself on the verge of tears. I didn't know whether weeping was allowed, but I didn't want to cry. I wanted to feel peace.

Each retreatant had a private meeting with Sharon, and when my turn came I told her about the sadness that was welling up in me, threatening to take over in an avalanche of tears. "What do I do about it?" I asked.

She pondered briefly and then simply said, "Try just observing it."

I looked at her for more instruction, she looked back at me with kindness. Apparently that was all she planned to say about it.

I went back to my mat in the middle of the hall, sat on my wooden kneeling bench, wrapped myself in a light blanket, and meditated, focusing on my breathing. Before long, thoughts crept into my mind, and there it was—the realization that this was my wedding anniversary, and that my marriage was dead, over, gone, and I wanted to sob.

Remembering Sharon's words, I observed my sadness. I noticed a lump in my throat, full of tears, rising, expanding, pressing, and threatening to force me to cry. As I observed it, the lump rose, and sure enough it reached my tear ducts and my eyes filled. A tear ran down my face, and then another.

And then . . . the lump receded, went back down my throat, and melted into the rest of me. It was over.

Is that all? I asked myself. *That couldn't have lasted more than a minute. That wasn't worth being afraid of!* Fearing a meltdown had consumed much more of my time and energy than had allowing the sadness.

I was looking forward to the next surge, to see if it would happen that way again. It did. For the remainder of the weekend, whenever I remembered that it was the anniversary of my failed marriage, the sadness rose, and I allowed it and observed it. It rose, I felt it, a tear or two overflowed, the lump receded, and it was over.

The lesson I learned that weekend was priceless, and I have since studied a great deal more about mindfulness meditation and Buddhism, which has become a central part of my spiritual practice, my coping mechanism, and my lifestyle.

Fortunately, bringing Buddhism into my life has not made it necessary to turn my back on any of the other rich bodies of wisdom and faith, such as Judaism and Universalism, all of which contain elements of strength and exist for the same purpose—to bring peace, courage, hope, and love to ourselves and others.

That spring I sold my piano in order to afford a kayak. Whenever time and weather allowed, I paddled the circumference of the pond, especially loving to drift under the gracefully arched branches of the old weeping willows, oaks, and maples overhanging the water. I could pretend I was an Indian maiden, making no sound, disturbing no wildlife. I named my kayak Minnehaha, because it sounded like a happy woman. Out on the pond I studied the water lilies and watched the birds in the woods around me and often thought about nothing at all, except the soundless movement of paddle and boat sliding through water. Kayaking on that pond hidden in the woods brought me closer and closer, each time, to finding the peace and healing I needed.

When I told a friend that I now had a kayak, he said, "It sounds like you've decided to follow that old adage, 'Love many, trust few, and paddle your own canoe.'"

I had never heard that before, but I liked it, and decided it was a good adage to follow.

Hope began to pierce my gloom. I decided to prepare for my new life. I still felt unattractive, dowdy, like the discard from a marriage that I was, and needed to feel better about my appearance before meeting new people. I hired a color consultant, a wardrobe consultant, and then a makeup coach, paying them all by credit card. Although I had always been responsible with money and knew I shouldn't be running up debt, I needed, and felt driven, to look good and feel good about myself. So I threw caution to the wind and considered the expenses an investment in my new life and future happiness.

After the consults and the ensuing shopping trips to buy the right makeup and clothes in the right colors, I was looking and feeling more attractive and self-confident.

"You know what you'd look good as?" my hairdresser said. "A blonde."

"No I wouldn't," I said. "I'd look terrible. I've tried on blonde wigs and couldn't stand how I looked in them."

"But your brunette color is faded, and you have more gray. Trust me. Let me do this, and if you don't like it, I'll strip it out and make you a faded brunette again."

Change had become what my life was all about. "O.K.," I said. "Go for it."

"You're gonna love it!" he said.

And I did.

I was the last to arrive at the regular monthly potluck lunch with my closest women friends, and all heads turned toward the door as I entered. A roar went up, and they applauded me. I felt gorgeous in my flattering clothes, soft fabrics in strong colors, tasteful makeup, and blonde hair. The group's opinion of my transformation seemed to be unanimous and enthusiastic. I could not have felt more acknowledged, more attractive, more ready to rejoin the world as the single woman I had become.

One Thursday after work I showered, grabbed a light supper, and dressed in a red silk shirtwaist dress with a shiny, black patent leather belt and matching shoes with little heels. I put on my new makeup, brushed my blonde hair, and headed off to someone's home for my first singles' event. My biggest fear was that everyone else would be much younger, and that despite all my refurbishing I would stand out as the oldest woman, and feel pitiful and out of place. But I had to go. I didn't yet know that being single can be fine, and I was afraid of being alone the rest of my life.

Dozens of people, women and men, welcomed me warmly, introducing themselves and inviting me to help myself to the snacks and beverages on the dining room table. To my relief, they all appeared to be about my age. A few reminded me that everyone had once been new there. They were extremely kind, making me feel comfortable, and I enjoyed the conversations and the evening.

Afterward, as people gathered up their coats, said their good-byes, and left, I had to hunt for my purse, and so I was the last to leave.

Almost the last. One man remained, and he walked me to my car. I had noticed him earlier. He was of average height, with a muscular build, olive skin, and short, curly silver hair, and behind his rimless glasses were the most magnetic green eyes I had ever seen. He introduced himself as I took in his velvety voice, warmth, and charm. His name was Nick. "It's cold, standing out here," he said. "Why don't we get in the car?" Before we said good night he had written down my phone number, held my hand for a while, and kissed me.

I drove home that night awash in feelings of warmth in places in my body that had been dormant for a long while. The next day something moved me to buy my first pair of silk panties. It was time for romance, and I felt ready.

He called two days later, and every day after that, and we quickly became lovers.

———

The first time Nick took me into his bed, with practiced off-handedness ("I feel like stretching out," he said, extending his hand to me. "Come, join me."), I felt excited but also awkward and scared. I had never been to bed with anyone but Paul, and I didn't know what it would be like with another man.

Nick knew exactly what to do and say. "Don't think," he whispered into my ear as he began to touch me. "Feel. Don't think.

38

Feel. Don't think. Feel . . . " until I was no longer sure which came first, feeling or not thinking. It was a mantra. *Feel. Don't think. Feel.*

I trusted him, figured he knew more about it than I did, so I followed his instructions. "Feel," I told myself. "Don't think. Feel," as I sank into the bliss of not thinking, only feeling, feeling pleasure, feeling loved, loved, loved, and I loved the feeling!

——— — — — ———

Nick taught me things I had never known—ways my body could move when aroused, how an orgasm could take over my self control and make me scream in ecstasy, how often I could experience it, how many ways there are to give and receive sexual pleasure. On the hottest afternoons of summer, he taught me that we could use baby powder all over our bodies to make love without sticking to each other—because our need to have sex was too strong to postpone until the weather cooled. He told me my breasts, which I had always thought were too small to be worthy of the name, were beautiful. "Are you sure you're forty-eight years old?" he teased. The more time I spent with him, the more beautiful and sexy I felt, and I was drawn into what I later learned was his exceptional appetite for sex, and came to feel I needed him. I became single-focused, and my focus became the same as his—sex. I forgot appointments and promises to my friends, I sneaked out of work, did whatever it took to be with him. He pointed out that what he did wasn't "having sex," it was "making love."

"You're in love with me," he said, and I believed him.

"It's all right," he said, "because I feel the same way. But don't ever ask me if I still love you. I'm telling you now, so you know."

And so I accepted that he loved me, and that I loved him.

My fantasies based on what I had seen and read in movies and romantic novels came to life. In Nick's arms I became the woman gliding across the dance floor whom others watched with admiration and envy. He glorified my body, encouraged me to wear skimpy shorts, revealing shirts, bikini bathing suits ("Be proud of your belly!") and made me feel like the sexiest and most beautiful woman alive. I was starving for this kind of validation, and he was a practiced expert. He nurtured and fed me, literally—cooking meals that he lay before me, something no man had ever done for me. Preparing and serving a meal has, all my life, seemed an act of love. I had been a vegetarian for ten years, but when he served me the only thing he knew how to make—meatloaf—I was so grateful to be fed by a man who loved me enough to cook for me that I ate it, and said good-bye to that part of who I had been.

———————

I happily confided everything to Grady. "He prepares the bed for me," I told her, "and when I take a shower he brings me towels, and then fixes me tea."

"He takes care of you," she summed up.

"Yes, and I can't remember the last time I felt taken care of."

"That's why you need it now."

"Yes," I admitted, "I need it now."

Although two years had passed since we separated, Paul hadn't done anything about the divorce. Nick told me that he didn't want to continue our relationship while I was still legally married. I was afraid of losing him, so I got a lawyer and started the process myself.

Nine

I took a trip with a friend from work, adding more debt to my credit cards, because I was still reveling in my autonomy and hungry for new things. I wanted Nick to come with me, but he said that while I was away he wanted to visit friends in Louisiana who were "a second family" to him.

I wanted to write to him, send picture postcards. "What address should I send them to?" I had asked him.

"Just hold onto them and bring them home with you," he said. "I'll read them when you get back."

I thought of him a lot while I was away, and held a mental image of him visiting with a family in Louisiana, perhaps an older couple with married kids and grandkids who would all be happy to see "Uncle Nick."

————————

When I returned from my trip, the marital house sold and it was time to go to court. Nick came along for moral support. In a few minutes, in the judge's chamber, a marriage of more than twenty-five years was ended. After the brief and unpleasant proceedings, Paul stopped me in the courthouse lobby and recited a speech that I couldn't understand. He spoke rapidly, something apparently rehearsed and formal, possibly about being sorry it had turned out this way and wishing me luck. And then he was gone.

————————

That night, when Nick came over, he said, "What do you think, is it time we live together? Maybe get married?"

I hadn't expected this. I was so stunned, all I could do was change the subject. The next morning I called him (he never stayed overnight, always left by three a.m., said he preferred waking up in the morning in his own surroundings) and said, "I'm sorry I couldn't answer you. But I think the fact that I couldn't speak is the answer. I'm not ready. I need time. I need to think about it. Is that all right with you? Can you wait for me to know, and give you my answer later?"

He said he would wait.

——— ——— ———

In Grady's office, most of the time now, we talked about Nick. He wouldn't tell me where he went or who he was with when he wasn't with me. I was deeply confused by his professions of love combined with his secrecy and separateness. Grady recommended I read some books about co-dependency, the patterns of trying to rescue people, as I had done with Paul, and of putting others' needs ahead of your own, as I was doing now with Nick. I read the books but I was so much like the women they described that I couldn't understand what they were doing wrong. Overlooking my needs for those of the man I loved seemed noble and good, not an illness. I didn't know any other way to love another, and I hadn't even begun to learn to love myself.

——— ——— ———

With my share of the proceeds from the sale of the marital home, I bought a cottage overlooking the pond in the same neighborhood where I had been renting. Nick looked at the house with me before I bought it, and he came with me to look at the furniture I was buying. I wanted the dining chairs to be comfortable for him and the couch big enough for him to lie down on.

The cottage had a cozy guest room with a skylight where the girls could stay with me whenever they wanted. They both were in college, now—Sasha was twenty and Becca, who had been awarded a scholarship, was eighteen. Each had a job and commuted to school, living with roommates nearby. They often did their laundry at my house, and we had meals at my table and took hikes around the pond, or kayaked or swam together. Our relationships were good again, strong and loving. They had grown apart from each other during their teen years, gone in separate directions, but were starting to become close again.

Nick showed up with a set of jewelers' measuring rings, and measured the fourth finger of my left hand. He started experimenting with how my first name would sound with his last name. The first time he spoke it, I fled from the room—so frightened of such a great change in my life. He said my new cottage home would be too small for all his things, and so we started driving around, scouting towns and neighborhoods, looking at houses and mobile homes. We joked about buying two mobile homes side by side, because he smoked heavily and I didn't smoke at all. Even though I hated cigarette smoke, I had come to associate the smell of his apartment, reeking of stale smoke, burned-down butts, and overflowing ashtrays, with sex, and it aroused me. I knew his smoking would become a problem when we married and lived together, but I felt too much in love with him to be realistic, and so I kept shopping with him for real estate.

We discovered that while I liked little houses, he wanted a large space for all his things, carpentry tools, and books. We agreed that what we needed was a small house with a huge barn, so we switched to looking at country real estate. Most weekends when the weather was nice, we'd pack a picnic and head out to a rural area, listening to music in the car, admiring the beautiful barns and covered bridges, and find a spot, preferably by a stream, to spread out our blanket, enjoy our lunch, and take photos of the countryside. Sometimes someone would offer to use our camera to take a picture of us, smiling, arms around each other's waists, the happy couple in love, house shopping in the country on a sunny weekend afternoon. It felt like a fantasy, the sort of thing that dreams and movies and wishes are made of.

———

I had always been a hard worker and a high achiever, and had quickly moved up in my job. I was now a manager, driving a brand new company car, earning the most I had ever earned. I dressed well and enjoyed my life of working, entertaining, living by the pond, and feeling loved.

But there was trouble in paradise. Nick disappeared at times, told me not to call him, and refused to spend significant occasions with me. I was so naïve, I believed his excuses—he needed the time to look for a job, he didn't approve of celebrating "Hallmark holidays," and so on. After one Saturday night I spent at home, hemming his new trousers and not knowing where he was, I questioned him the next day and found out that he had gone to a singles dance.

I told him I didn't understand why he would go to a singles dance, if we were a couple.

His response was, "Oh, you're not going to complain about that, are you? Don't make a big deal out of it. I just wanted to get out for a few hours and see my friends. Those people have been my friends since long before I met you."

That was true, he had been single for twenty years and had spent them going to singles dances. All the regulars there knew him. So I figured, because he insisted, that I was being unreasonable, and a nag, I didn't own him, and he had the right to spend an evening with his friends. I still hadn't learned that my own thoughts and feelings were valid, and I didn't realize that he was treating me badly by excluding me from another part of his life. He said he was committed to our relationship, but when I asked him what "committed" meant to him, he became annoyed with my question and dismissed it.

I didn't like or understand his behavior, but when I asked him about it he silenced me with, "You ask too many questions." I was so used to being told, first by my parents, then my husband, and now Nick, that my thinking was wrong, that I figured relationships were simply this difficult, and that my jealousy and suspicion were weaknesses in me.

I had tried to discuss monogamy with him, but he insisted that it was something wonderful if it happened by chance, to be appreciated as a bonus rather than an obligation. His double-talk meant "no" but I couldn't hear it because he wasn't saying it. Foolishly, I hoped he meant "maybe," "yes," or "in time."

"Love is enough," he always insisted. I was confused and wondered whether I was crazy, because I felt something was wrong in our relationship, but he told me I was asking for too much. The red warning flags were flying, but I wasn't seeing them.

Having been in a monogamous marriage for more than twenty-five years, I had missed the sexual revolution of the '60s and '70s and no longer knew "the rules." I asked Steve, who had been single all the time that I was married, what the rules were for being in relationships.

He said, "There are no rules anymore."

"Then how do I know what to do, not do?"

"You decide what you like and want," Steve said, "and those become your rules. Then you try to find someone whose rules match yours." Nick's rules didn't match mine, but I couldn't pull myself away from him.

Wild with frustration at his waving away my questions, for the first time in my life I started snooping. I saw in his checkbook register that he was writing monthly checks to a woman I hadn't met, whose name I had seen on a postcard on his bookcase. I confronted him. He told me she was one of his longtime friends, part of his "second family," the one in Louisiana. "She's really strapped for money," he said, "and has helped me out when I needed it, so I send her a little to help her out."

A few months later she came up from New Orleans to visit, and he told me not to call and that he wouldn't have time for me, because he would be busy showing her around. If I'd had a shred of sense I would have admitted that his excluding me meant he was doing something unfair to either her or me, and I'd have broken it off with him. But by that time, I was as addicted to him as he was to me, and I stayed away, never met her, and was back in his bed a week later, after she left.

I dated other men and didn't tell Nick, partly to get even, but also because I wanted to get out and have fun when I couldn't be with him.

I ran a personal ad in a city newspaper, the best resource at that time for meeting and dating. I waited for responses, but none came.

Not being one to give up easily, I called the paper's office and asked, "Did my ad really pull in no responses at all?"

"Hmmm," the woman on the phone said, "you live in Jamaica Plain, right?"

"No." I said. "Not anywhere near there."

"Oh-oh," she said.

"So . . . responses to my ad went to someone else?"

"I'm sorry," she said. "It happens sometimes. I'll tell you what we can do for you. Write an ad of any length, give it a headline if you want, and we'll run it for as long as you want, at no cost."

This was good luck landing in my lap. I spent days composing the catchiest ad I could think of. *SPRING CHICKEN*, read the headline, and the body of the ad read something like this:

> Mature, attractive, tiny blonde with *joie de vivre* seeks nonsmoking man of wit and intelligence for dating and perhaps more. Interests include music, especially jazz and classical, easy hikes, kayaking, cross-country skiing, fireworks on the Fourth of July, and meaningful conversation about books, history, psychology. Enjoys laughter, fine food, and travel. Please write.

45

This time responses poured in, and by the fourth week I had to call the paper to cancel the ad. I had enough dates to keep me busy for months, and I'd never get through the pile of letters from wonderful-sounding men to call them all. I met nice men, and had many dates with younger men and older, for dancing, dining, and concerts.

But if Nick was available, I needed to be with him. Neither of us could stop what had become an obsession, in which we both were bound to each other by hunger and love, although we couldn't meet each other's primary needs—mine for commitment and truth, his for freedom and privacy. I believed I was lucky that someone loved me, and I didn't know I deserved to be treated better than he was treating me. The sexual pull between us was impossible to resist, and it prevented me from having those feelings for anyone else.

Every day I still asked myself whether I would accept his proposal of marriage. It had been almost a year since he had first mentioned it, two years since we had met and fallen in love, and I rationalized that if we were married, then he would promise me, and give me, the things that were missing—vacations and New Year's Eve together, the assurance of monogamy, no secrets, and no lies.

Ten

Nick told me he was going to Louisiana to visit his friend, and I offered to drive him to the airport. I prepared a little surprise for him, cutting out crossword puzzles from his favorite newspaper every day, and the solutions that appeared the following day, and pasting them into a notebook—puzzles in the front of the book, solutions at the back—so he could enjoy his favorite pastime on the plane.

I also set up an appointment to see a lawyer during the week he'd be away, to find out what impact marriage to him would have on my finances. If I could be assured that my home and income could not be taken to satisfy his unpaid student loans, I intended to say yes, and marry him.

I hadn't told Grady yet, because at some level I knew that when I spoke it, my plan would sound foolish, even to me. I wanted to hold onto my fantasy. The last time Grady and I met, and I had agonized about the relationship with Nick and the stress it caused me, she said, "It sounds awfully expensive, Sam."

"What do you mean?" I asked.

"Well, is what you get from the relationship worth what it takes out of you?"

It was a sobering question, and a hard call to make. Was the relationship costing me more than it gave me? Probably. But I clung to the thought that marriage would tip the scale. If we were married he would give me the assurance he had been withholding, and then the relationship would be fair, even positive, and happy for both of us.

The night before he left I was at his apartment, planning to sleep over for an early rising, to make his flight time. "Please leave me the phone number where I can reach you if I need to," I said.

To my surprise, he left the room. I followed him into the bedroom. "Look," he said, "I can't give you the number. You can't call me there."

"Why not?" I was still so unsuspecting, so needy and naïve regarding relationships, so deeply in denial about this one.

He turned and went back to the living room. I followed.

"Because," he said, "her heart would break if she knew about you." With that, he left again for the bedroom, and I followed him.

"But . . ." I was bewildered, " . . . what will you tell her when we get married? Aren't you going to have to tell her about me then?"

Back to the living room, he in the lead. He finally stopped and said, "I can't marry you."

"Why not?" I couldn't break through my innocence and avoidance of the truth.

"Because I have commitments and obligations."

"To whom?"

"To her," he said.

I cast about for my next words. "But . . . you asked me to marry you! We've been talking about marriage for a year!"

"I don't remember," he said, and that was his way out, the passive-aggressive hammer that slams down onto any conversation and ends it.

"You don't remember? You came to my house and said—"

He shook his head and returned to the bedroom. I grabbed my coat and headed out the door, to my car, and home. I didn't sleep that night, I just tossed, and stared at the dark, and tried to make sense of what had happened.

In the morning I rose early, took the gift-wrapped notebook of puzzles, and showed up at his door three hours before flight time. I couldn't speak, and all he could do was look at me. We both had tears rolling down our faces. I drove him to the airport, still not speaking, and when I dropped him off in front of the terminal, I slipped a note into his pocket wishing him a safe flight, what I would have said if I could speak.

For the rest of the weekend I talked and cried with Steve, who had been aware all along of my twisted relationship with Nick. By Tuesday I understood that Nick had gone to enormous lengths to make me believe, really believe, that we were going to marry, apparently only as a way to keep me tied to him, and in his bed. I had allowed myself to be deceived, and given my heart and two years of my life to a man who had lied to me and used me to cheat on the primary woman in his life, with my full permission and my misplaced trust. I had seen plenty of evidence that he had no compunctions about lying to others, I just didn't, in my naïveté, ever think he would lie so outrageously to me.

By the time I went to bed on Tuesday night, my shock was giving way to anger, but I needed more time to process the whole two wonderful years of romance and promise that were changing into something else, something humiliating and cruel. I decided that when he came home at the end of the week I would not be at the airport to pick him up. I would have all the things he had kept at my house— some socks and underwear, a sweater, a suit, shirt, and tie—piled neatly on the floor in front of his door, with the key to his apartment in an envelope on top, and no note. Afflicted with lifelong habits of politeness and restraint, I didn't even consider dumping it all in a heap, making him bend down over and over again and fold all the clothes himself, or just burning them instead of returning them.

A full moon was rising that night, an event that was usually of great interest to me, but I didn't pay attention to it. My mind was still working on my anger, surprise, humiliation, and determination to never see or speak to him again.

Eleven

I jolted awake, sprang from my bed. *What happened?* The room was flooded with moonlight. *What woke me up?* There hadn't been a sound. The carpet was soft and cool under my bare feet. I glanced at the clock on the maple nightstand. Midnight. I stepped to the open window. The May night air was warm. The full moon, huge and gleaming white, poured silver light onto the street, the rooftops, the grassy lawns, and glinted on the pond. The world outside was bright as day, but the doors and gates of the houses and yards up and down the street were closed, the windows dark, the neighborhood still and silent.

Something was wrong. I felt agitated, craved soothing, but I was alone. Going back to sleep felt impossible. I hurried to the maple dresser, the room so light I didn't need to turn on the lamp, and rummaged through the bracelets and necklaces in my jewelry box until my fingers closed around the hammered silver circle and chain a silversmith had made for me, a little bigger than a quarter, curved like a segment of a sphere, and with an uneven surface. My moon, my good luck charm. Without knowing why, but knowing I had to do something and maybe this was it, I placed the shiny disc, now reflecting the moonlight in the room, just below my collarbone, in the open neck of my pink, cotton nightgown and, with trembling fingers, fastened the delicate chain behind my neck.

There. I placed my hand on the amulet and returned to the window. I have always loved the moon in all her phases, but the full moon has been the one that reaches deepest into my heart, making me giddy, excited, euphoric. But that night I was restless, confused, and feeling strange. *What is it, Moon?* I thought. *What are you telling me?*

I climbed back into bed. With my hands against my chest, lightly fingering the silver disc, I eventually dozed, moonlight still pouring through the window. In a few hours I would be awakened by the pounding of the brass knocker against the door and Paul, bringing his terrible news.

Two days later, when Sasha told someone that her sister had been killed at midnight, he asked her, "Did your mother have a premonition?" She told me this while we walked around the pond at dawn on the day of the funeral.

A couple of nights before, Nick had sneaked out of the house of the woman in New Orleans to call me. I was paying a condolence call on the parents of one of the other victims of the crash and wasn't at home; my friends were gathered at my house, and Steve answered the phone. I was told afterward that when Steve realized Nick didn't know about Becca's death, he told him.

Nick was incredulous, swore furiously, caught between me in my hour of greatest need and the woman who couldn't know about me. "Tell her I'll call again in a few days," was the message Nick gave Steve.

Steve figured Nick hadn't heard him. "Becca's dead," he repeated. "The funeral is Thursday."

"Yeh," Nick said. "Tell Sam I'll call her in a few days."

After he hung up, I was told, Steve paced my kitchen floor punching his open palm and shouting, "He'll call her in a few days! He'll call her in a few days! What kind of a boyfriend says he'll call her in a few days!"

What kind of a boyfriend? A good question, with an answer that was now becoming obvious.

———

Steve had driven me to the funeral home to see Becca, a beautiful, life-sized doll with long blonde hair and lots of makeup, shrouded in white satin and covered below her shoulders with a white satin sheet that matched the lining of her polished pine casket, so I couldn't see her broken body. I had needed to see her, be sure it was her, and so breaking with the Jewish tradition of immediate burial, I had asked to have her body restored from the condition in which it had been found, so that I could bear to look at her.

The funeral director had bragged, "That was the hardest job of reconstruction I've ever had to do!"

"Don't tell me that," I snapped. "I'm her *mother*."

I had carefully avoided touching her skin, dreading how I knew it would feel, cold, not the soft, warm, velvet skin I knew so well.

51

Instead, I brushed her spray-stiffened hair with the backs of my fingers and whispered, "Rest, Darling."

I did not know yet that for many years afterward I would have dreams that she was alive somewhere and needed me, and I was not there for her. I would drag myself awake thinking, *I must go to her and help her, and beg her forgiveness!* And then I would remember that she was dead, that I had seen her dead. I could never decide which was worse, dreaming she was still alive and that I was not part of her life, or knowing that she was dead. Both hurt, hurt beyond belief, and I would drag myself about the business of my day feeling sick in my body, my head throbbing, for hours afterward, every time.

I would also call Steve in about six months to ask, "That was Becca we saw in the casket, wasn't it?" I had begun to wonder whether, perhaps, a mistake had been made.

He paused, then said slowly, "Yes, it was Becca."

I walked now with Sasha on our usual, favorite path around the pond, this time not talking much, each of us grappling with our own thoughts and memories, and trying to take in the new reality. I was weak and lightheaded from shock, lack of sleep, and the loss of several pounds in the past two days. I hadn't been able to eat a thing, but losing so much weight had to be due to more than two days of not eating, it had to be the emotional pain and grief.

I looked at Sasha and she looked at me, we made eye contact, and I wanted to blurt out, "Thank God I still have you!" I couldn't say it, afraid it would sound as though she meant more to me than Becca, but I know she saw the message in my eyes, and her eyes said back, "Thank God I'm still here with you!"

I had been trying to remember Becca beyond the first week of her life, and had managed to bring my memory farther forward in time, to when she was about three or four. I remembered dancing with her in my arms in the living room to the music we liked, and playing the piano for the girls after they were tucked into bed, so the music would waft up the stairs to them. Becca loved it and always asked for more.

At the end of a trail through the trees that led to the pond's edge, Sasha and I stood where the water lapped at the rocks. With a barely audible flap, a Great Blue Heron rose from the pond grasses, its majestic wings extended, and gracefully glided above the water to the opposite shore, where it disappeared into the tall grass again. "This," I announced, "shall now and forever be Rebecca's Memorial Spot."

Although I thought about marking the place, maybe getting a small plaque to nail to the trunk of one of the huge, old trees, I knew I didn't need to. For me, this spot by the pond would always exist and be about Becca, and I would remember it even if I never came here again, if the trees fell into the water, or bulldozers ripped them out to make room for a new waterfront property.

My "Velcro memory," as I called it, which was becoming a plague, a monster, holding onto everything that had ever touched it and increasingly taking over my thoughts, stretching back a lifetime and already packed with so much of her life, my life, our family as it used to be, the horrible years at the end of my marriage, Nick's crushing betrayal—Nick, who would not be at the funeral because he was a thousand miles away with another woman—would easily stretch a tiny bit farther and take in this moment, and this spot, too.

Twelve

My father and I had one of our classic arguments just before the funeral. I had walked away from him earlier when he started asking Sasha about her finances and her car, and my mother about the food for the people who would arrive after the service. But a short while later, as we sat in the back yard awaiting the limousine that would take us to the cemetery, he turned to me and began to ask his usual questions about how much this was going to cost, and whether there was enough food, and I exploded at him.

"Don't you understand," I raged, standing to face him, my fists clenched in frustration, "that I have just lost my *daughter?*"

"I know," he said sadly, lowering his head. "She's my granddaughter."

My rage dissolved. "Then *why*," I implored, "are you talking to me about money and food?"

He looked up and said softly, "I'm just trying to distract you."

"Oh," I said, more calm now, "is *that* it? *Distract* me? Dad, you can't distract me. I don't want to be distracted. It's taking every bit of energy I have to draw each breath, to take each step. I can't add anything to my plate or think about anything."

He apologized, and I did, too.

"Are we O.K. then?" I asked.

"We've always been O.K.," he said.

I hadn't known that we had always been O.K. I had only known that he had always driven me crazy with what I thought were his obsessions with money, food, and cars. I suddenly realized he had motives of kindness that I had never understood. It was a gift, that day, to finally understand that my father's maddening ways could be motivated by his caring.

When we arrived at the cemetery, three large groups of people stood waiting on separate spots beneath the tall oaks and maples and flowering dogwood trees. "There seem to be two other funerals going on at the same time," I remarked. But as Sasha, Paul, my parents, and I stepped out of the limousine, all three groups converged to surround and greet us quietly.

The day was as picture-perfect as a calendar photo for the month of May, or a movie set for a Disney film—brilliant, with bright-green spring grass and a cloudless blue sky, and the air was warm and soft against my skin and fragrant with lilacs. I felt detached, like an actress on a stage, gliding through my role. I had very few lines—"Thank you, thank you for coming,"—and I accepted hugs and then walked holding hands with Sasha and my mother across the grass to the spot where Becca's coffin waited.

In a black silk dress I had bought a few weeks earlier for parties and dancing, I sat at one end of the small row of folding chairs the funeral staff had placed beside the open grave. Sasha stood beside me and held my hand. Paul, doubled over, ashen-faced, and looking very old, sat between my mother and me, and my father sat at the other end. The hundreds of family, friends, neighbors, and co-workers who had come formed a huge circle around us and the casket, which was adorned with a spray of yellow roses and suspended above the grave. As the service began, Paul grabbed my free hand and my mother's, on either side of him, and gripped them tightly.

Paul and I had planned the funeral in keeping with our liberal beliefs, to honor Becca and meet the needs of our families and our friends as well as our own. The minister from our church and the rabbi from Mark's temple began alternately reading from the Psalms. I was a mannequin, numb, without reaction or emotion. I didn't cry, because I couldn't. When the rabbi asked us to stand to recite Kaddish, the prayer for the dead, I felt Dennis, standing behind me, slip his arms under mine and lift me to my feet. I stood dumbly until he put his hands on my shoulders and gently pushed me back down to my seat.

I couldn't keep my attention on what was being recited from the prayer books, and as the service continued I looked around the circle, checking every face. *Linda is here*, I noted. *And Robert. And Margie. And Jim.* When my eyes reached Dan, the president of the company where I worked, he was looking at me and waiting for my eyes to reach his, and he nodded to me, a warm unspoken acknowledgment of me that I appreciated. My gaze moved on until I had completed the circle.

I had written a eulogy and asked the minister to read it, because I knew I would be unable to say the words aloud. Digging deep into my memories the night before, I still couldn't remember Becca past the age of about three or four, and so I had written about that.

"These are the words of Samantha, Rebecca's mother," the minister said, "which she has asked me to read."

"If I had only one word to sum up what Becca was like," he read, "it would be *gentle*. One day when she was very little, not yet in school, our parakeet, Biliverdin, was sick. Biliverdin is a medical term for a green pigment, and we had named him Biliverdin, "Billy" for short, because he was green. The poor little bird was flapping his wings, thrashing around in his cage, his neck drooping at an alarming angle. The vet told me to bring him in right away.

"'Becca,' I said to her, stooping down to her height to watch her face, 'I have a very important job for you to do. We need to get Billy to the vet, and someone needs to hold him while I drive. Can you do that?'

"She said yes.

"'The important thing,' I explained, 'is that you hold him with your hands closed, so that he can't fly away, but you mustn't squeeze him, because his bones are tiny and they could break.'

"She had sat beside me, a little girl too young to be in school, and held him tenderly in her cupped hands, all the way to the vet. What a remarkable feat for a child so young, to understand what the sick bird needed from her! But that was Becca, always tender and gentle, never hurting anyone or anything, all her life.

"I will always remember, all of us who knew her will remember, her gentleness."

After reading my eulogy, the minister read Paul's. I was grateful for what Paul had written, that if she had lived, she would have made it out of the confused state of her late adolescence and become successful at whatever she chose to do.

All through the service a red-tailed hawk hovered and wafted high above us, as if observing and listening. I watched Becca's coffin lowered into the ground and stood to toss dirt into her grave, a common practice which I had requested, to indicate that we were burying one of our own. I heard the soft brushing sound made by the dirt landing on the polished wood, and sang under my breath, "Bye, bye, Baby, remember you're my baby . . . "

Then everyone lined up to toss more dirt onto her coffin, to symbolize that they were helping us bury her. When the ritual ended

56

the hawk flew away, and I stood as people lined up again, this time to pay their respects.

I politely and warmly thanked them all and invited them back to my home. I was cool and ladylike, no feeling, no crying, no wailing and keening and falling down, or throwing myself into the open grave, all of which I thought of and wished I could do, but it was all locked away inside me and I couldn't let it out, because I could not let this be real. I still remember most of all that the day was warm and bright and beautiful, and full of love, and yet it was the darkest day of my life.

Then I went home in the big, black limousine and waited for Becca to come up the front walk, enter the house smiling, hug me, and say, "Hi, Mom!"

My mother asked, "Where is Nick?" He had visited my parents with me, brought my mother flowers, and they had entertained him at dinner, given him gifts—a plant stand for his apartment, theater tickets for us.

"In Louisiana," was all I said.

She looked both questioning and disapproving. "He belongs here, at your side," she said.

That's what I thought, too, but I was too humiliated, angry, and heartbroken by his absence to respond. I appreciated her saying it, though, because she validated my sense of what was reasonable for me to expect from Nick.

He did call in a few days, but I was too numb to hear or remember the conversation. He returned on his scheduled flight at the end of the week, after the funeral, and showed up at my house the following morning. Only Sasha and I were at home. I was in my bedroom. I didn't want to see him, but he wouldn't leave. I didn't want him to touch me, but he put his arms around me and pulled me down onto the bed. I punched him and yelled, surprising him. He had never known me to be angry or resisting. After he had left with his little pile of neatly folded clothes and shaving gear, Sasha and I walked around the pond in silence, each of us privately struggling to figure out how to go on when so much had changed.

Part II

Searching

Thirteen

Love—not food, and certainly not sleep—sustained me. I had come home from the funeral to find Marilyn at my kitchen stove, and Paul's cousins spreading the table with a buffet for the crowd that trooped home with me from the cemetery. The living room was fragrant and alive with flowers, giant baskets of fruit stood on the kitchen counters and the floor, and the refrigerator was packed with food to take me through the weeks ahead. I moved through the scene like a zombie, in a state of shock that would last for months.

For the next few days my little cottage overflowed with people—co-workers, neighbors, longtime friends I hadn't seen in years, and family, quietly coming and going, bringing food and plants. I was treated like an injured fledgling, cradled in fluffy cotton, spoken to softly, handled gently.

Paul held court in the kitchen, I in the living room, so guests could pay respects to us both. He didn't speak to me unless I spoke first. At one point I sat surrounded by friends, one with her arm around me, another holding my hand, the others bathing me with the softness in their eyes. I put my head back onto the sofa cushions and said, "It feels so wonderful to have you all here, so close. Thank you."

When flashes of anger penetrated my numbness, I reverted to my habit of speaking softly, afraid to unleash my dark side. This habit had often puzzled others who would say, "Why didn't you tell us you were angry?" and I would say, "I did!" and they would respond, "That was anger? I had no idea you were really upset."

During those few days following Becca's death I spoke to my friends in a whisper so low they had to draw close to hear me. "I'm so angry!" I whispered, clenching my fists. "I'm angry at God for letting Becca die. I'm angry at Becca for dying. And most of all I'm angry at Nick, for not being here for me." Being angry at Nick was easiest because he was responsible for his choices.

My friends understood and agreed.

But then the house emptied of visitors and I was alone, still waiting for Becca to come home. When she didn't, I waited for her to call, growing increasingly angry as days and then weeks passed and the call never came. *O.K., Becca,* I thought, *Enough! This joke has gone on too long. Call me, apologize, and come back!* I alternately railed and withdrew, flashing with rage at whoever came to mind and then pulling my anger deep inside myself. My chest, my arms, my stomach, all hurt, and I wasn't sleeping well. I felt a cold wind blowing through a hole in my chest big enough for a cannonball. Each time I looked down and saw no gaping wound, no puddle of blood at my feet, I was dumbfounded.

A pair of thick lead doors, held shut by heavy chains and iron bars, lurked in my brain. Some terrible truth, too awful to comprehend, pressed from behind them, occasionally seeping out through a paper-thin space at the bottom, and the doors were threatening to burst open, to let it pour out. Whenever I looked at them, I shivered with fear and quickly looked away.

The regular monthly potluck with my women friends was going to meet at my house, and I couldn't remember who usually provided the wine. Ashamed that my brain was failing me, I called a woman in the group.

"The hostess provides the wine," she said. "But I'll be happy to pick it up for you on my way to your house."

"Thanks," I said. "That would be great."

A week later she called me. "Why didn't you just ask me to pick up the wine for you," she asked, "instead of pretending you didn't know who was supposed to provide it?"

"I really didn't remember," I said, humiliated.

"Oh, come on," she said. "I don't believe you can't remember something we've been doing the same way for ten years."

I couldn't convince her. I was not only crushed by her disbelief, but also terrified that my brain was permanently damaged, would never work right again.

I was afraid to leave the house to shop for groceries because I might meet someone I knew who would ask me, "What's new?" and I'd have to tell them about Becca.

Nick kept calling and coming over, although I had told him we were through. He found excuses to see me, stopping by the house to deliver something he had bought for me—a quart of milk, a rose—ringing the doorbell and asking to use the bathroom. Weak from grieving, I had no resistance.

On the day the food in the refrigerator and cupboards finally ran out, the phone rang. It was Nick, and I burst into tears.

"I have no food," I told him, "and I'm afraid to go to the store."

"Make a list of the things you need," he said, "and I'll be there in twenty minutes."

He took me shopping, pushing the cart, shepherding me up and down the aisles, staying close to me, and brought me home and helped put the groceries away before he left for his job on the night shift.

The next time I needed to go to the market I found the courage to drive the short distance myself—and got lost coming home. Another day I tried to enter a familiar highway interchange to drive south, used the wrong ramp, ended up driving north, took the next exit to reverse direction, and drove up and down the highway, choosing wrong exits, for a half hour, weeping. I knew there was something very wrong going on, but I couldn't figure out what it was.

I did not yet know the word trauma.

Nick showed up at my door and found me crying. I let him in, let him hold me. Wordlessly, he took the afghan from the sofa and spread it on the carpeted floor. I melted into his arms and let him undress me, and he made love to me on the living room floor, just inside the front door, while I clung to him and wept. He taught me another new thing about sex that day—that it could let me know, more powerfully than anything else, that I was alive. I could feel. Just because Becca had died didn't mean I had died, too.

Not that I didn't want to be dead—I had considered suicide seriously, but only briefly. Sasha had lost what I had lost—our family, our home, her sister—and I couldn't take me away from her, too. I was trapped. I had to find a way to endure living.

Sasha told me later that she had wanted to die, too, and all that kept her from killing herself was not wanting to inflict that additional loss upon me.

63

A movie started in my mind, an endless loop, projected onto the inside of my skull, that wouldn't stop. It showed the last ninety seconds of Becca's life, according to the information I had been given.

She is in the back seat of a shiny, green, hardtop sedan being driven too fast by someone who is very drunk. The night sky is lit up by the full moon. Suddenly, at the fork between two highways, the car goes up onto the guardrail. She sits up straight, terror stricken. The front of the car hits the big, blue sign by the side of the highway with a loud bang, and then the deafening screech of metal as the sign rips the roof off and the car continues to sail upward. Her pretty, young face turns white, she gasps. The car flips over. She and two others in the car are thrown, she to the right, the others to the left. My movie camera follows her as she soars upward through the air and over the embankment, and then down, down into the deep gully between the two highways. I see her face, her wide open mouth, her blue-gray eyes unblinking. The only sound is wind rushing past, then a deep, long scream (hers? mine?), followed by a monstrous thud that I can feel, mixed with the crackle of bones breaking, and then silence, except for the faraway crunching and tinkling of glass and murmur of people's voices up above her, on the highway, where someone lies pinned in the wreckage and two others lie motionless on the moonlit pavement. Soon, sirens, as police and ambulances arrive. She is alone, down here in the gully, where it is quiet, until later, when she will be found.

The movie ended there, but started right up again, from the beginning. It ran to the end and played again. And again, for months. There were so many things I couldn't know that tortured me. What did her terror feel like? Did it occur to her to wonder whether we would ever find her? Did she see the ground, far below, rushing toward her, or had she gone into merciful shock? Did she feel the impact of the ground or did she die of fright before that happened? I wanted so much to stop the movie or tune it out, but I couldn't.

As more months went by, it played on and off, whenever it wanted to, for the next year or so. I was unable to concentrate on anything, unable to work, barely able to breathe and walk, and get from morning to night, day to day. Every time her body made impact with the ground, I broke apart inside, as if I had been the one who had been thrown and fallen so far and been smashed to bits. It's called vicarious trauma, experiencing indirectly the brutality done to someone else. As my children's mother, I had always physically felt the pains of their injuries, and now I was feeling the violence of Becca's death.

And so about six months after she died I finally fell apart, crumbled inside, felt like a porcelain vase that had been pushed off a roof and smashed into a million pieces on the ground. Mentally and emotionally, I had absorbed her experience, and it had become mine. I could either lie there, demolished and useless, or painstakingly put myself back together again. But I didn't know how to do that, and I had no energy to try.

I poured my heart out to Grady, who listened closely, tenderly, as I wept about the movie and about Nick and expressed my despair and struggled with my grief. My thoughts flew out of control and I told everyone I met that my daughter had died—maybe so that I could hear it, begin to understand and believe it.

A fence builder I had called before Becca's death was sitting at my kitchen table, calculating the price of a new fence for my backyard.

"My daughter was killed," I blurted out.

He looked up and said, "Mine, too."

Oh! This would be someone who understood!

"Three years ago this Sunday," he said. "It was on her birthday."

"I'm so sorry!" I said, realizing he had hurt this much, too. "Tell me," I ventured, "I think I'm beginning to catch on. The pain—" and here I placed my arm across my chest, hand on my heart, and tapped my chest with a closed fist, "—the pain doesn't go away, does it?"

He placed his arm across his chest, tapped the same spot with his fist, and said, "No, it doesn't go away. You learn to live with it."

In that moment a new door in my mind was opened, and I grasped something that would make life easier. What he had said was about the *possible*. Learning to live with it felt more possible than making the pain go away.

It was the single most valuable bit of advice I ever received.

Fourteen

In time, relatives and friends drifted back to whatever they had been doing. Some of them grew tired of my grief, which was lasting longer than they had thought it would.

A good friend who had stayed close by my side throughout the week of the funeral and long afterward asked me to meet her at a restaurant for lunch.

"Sam," she said, after we had ordered, chatted, and begun to eat, "being with you is very difficult. How much longer are you going to be depressed?"

"I have no idea," I told her. "I've never been through this before."

"Well," she said, "I can't take much more of it. I've done all I could for you, and I thought that would help you get over it, but I never expected that being your friend would mean having to watch this much pain."

It was true, she had done a lot for me—stayed at my house when Becca was killed, been a buffer between me and the outside world, and then invited me to her house so I wouldn't be alone.

"People tell me it takes a year," I said, "and it's been only half that. I just don't know. I can't promise what will happen; it's not in my control."

"Well," she said, putting her fork down, "I can't wait to find out how long it lasts. I can't take any more. I thought you'd be over it by now, and it hurts too much to watch you." She reached for her purse and I sensed she was about to leave.

"But this is what friendship is," I protested. "Haven't you ever been comforted and held up by a friend?"

"No, I've always made sure I didn't need anyone to comfort me, or hold me up." She reached into her purse.

"Then this is an opportunity for you to experience the kind of friendship where friends stand by each other," I said. "Now it's my turn to need support, but when it's yours, I'll be there for you."

"I don't intend to need it," she said. "And I just can't give you any more." She stood up, put money down beside her plate to pay her share of the lunch, and left. I sat at the table stunned, weeping, as the waiter brought the check and I paid, then left the restaurant and drove home, feeling I had been hit hard while I was down. Her help had been generous and steady, which made the loss of it greater. Now I had lost not only Becca, but my good friend, too.

More friends let me know that I was not pleasant or interesting or fun to be with anymore, or just stopped returning my calls. I still had Grady. Steve stayed, and Marilyn and Mike, and Nick.

I couldn't get rid of Nick. He came when no one else did, took me out for ice cream cones, took me to the botanical gardens, where we walked beneath the flowering crabapple trees casting their pink light and filling my head with their fragrance that reminded me of Becca and the crabapple tree we'd had in our backyard when she was growing up. He continued to show up at my door with gifts, and used every excuse possible to see me and to waken me with his lovemaking. He made love to me often, in many places—outdoors, indoors on the rugs, the furniture, in every room, even in public places, hiding behind walls, in dark places, unseen by people nearby—and I couldn't stop him, because if I ever needed to feel loved, feel the intimate closeness of another, and to feel validation of my worth and life, I never needed it more than then.

So I filled his insatiable need for sex, and he filled my need to feel alive, not dead. He still called it love. Maybe he did love me, but for me it was now something else. It had become my drug, my addiction, and I was using him as he had used me. Our "lovemaking" may have been only an illusion, a temporary balm on my wounded heart, but it felt like a lifeline, and I grabbed on.

Fifteen

Rio Caliente, "hot river," runs through a valley in Mexico, filling the pools at the spa where my friend Betty worked. "I think it would be good if you came down," she said. "It can be a very healing place, and you would be my guest." She said she would provide my room and board, and there were always my credit cards to pay for the low airfare she recommended. I was charging everything these days, and the debt was mounting, but I was desperate for the healing Betty offered. Because I couldn't think clearly, she told me which airline to fly from Boston, where to stay when I arrived in Guadalajara, and what to tell the taxi driver who would take me to the spa near Mount Tequilla, an extinct volcano.

I spent two weeks of my vacation time on the mountainside, in a comfortable, private, adobe *casita*, hiked with Betty, and discovered chunks of fossilized volcanic rock—something I had never seen before—scattered over the ground in the forest. I lazed in the sun, soaked in the pools, took siesta several times a day, and enjoyed a return to vegetarian cuisine.

On my first evening there the group around the dinner table talked into the night, and the conversation made its way to drinking and the funny things people say and do when they've had too much to drink. I was still thinking of alcohol as my daughter's killer—alcohol, and the person who had been drunk at the wheel. I suddenly couldn't stand the conversation, but wasn't sure how to end it.

I stood up. "I'm sorry," I said, "but I can't handle this. I need to go back to my room and call it a night."

I trembled and wept in my room for a while, and finally fell asleep. In the morning I asked Betty whether I had been rude, and she reassured me that I had handled it well and no one was offended.

I realized that from now on I was going to be seeing things through new eyes, filtering everything through my altered experience.

To this day, I cannot find anything humorous about drunkenness, and I can't imagine that I ever will.

———————

Betty took me to a nearby town for a sunny, pleasant day of browsing, shopping, and lunch at an outdoor café. Our first stop was a jewelry shop where I bought silver bangle bracelets to bring home as gifts. The jeweler, seeing an opportunity to sell me more, pulled out trays of earrings, necklaces, and charms, and asked cheerfully, "Do you have daughters?"

His question hit me like a brick. Do I have daughters? Did I? This was the first time anyone had asked me that since Becca died. I didn't know the answer.

The jeweler grew tired of waiting for me to respond and walked away. But I couldn't move, I stood there still contemplating the question. I needed the answer.

Finally, very slowly, I heard each word emerge from my mouth.

"Yes," I said, and paused.

(*Yes, I do, I thought.*)

"I. Have."

(*I paused to search for the next word.*)

"A." (*That's the word.*)

"Daughter." (*Singular.*)

For years that question would challenge me hundreds of times—at the hairdresser's while someone was shampooing or cutting my hair and trying to make conversation, or at social gatherings of people standing around with drinks in their hands, casting about for things to talk about. "Do you have children?" An innocent, friendly question.

I would try answering different ways. If I said I had one daughter, I felt as though I was erasing Becca's life. I couldn't do that, so I would say "daughters."

"How many?" people would ask.

"Two."

People asked, "How old are they?"

I would say, "My older girl is twenty-four."

And they would ask, "And the younger?"

And so I was always brought back to that place in the conversation, having to answer. I tried, "If she had lived, she would be twenty-two," but that was meaningless. Becca wasn't twenty-two and never would be. "She died at twenty," I felt forced to say.

Some people were kind enough to say, "I'm so sorry," and change the subject. But others would say, "Oh! How did that happen?"

At first, I found myself telling people the story line of the movie in my head, struggling with each word as it fought my resistance to speak it. Eventually I learned to say, "I'm afraid that's my least favorite topic of conversation," and they would say, "Oh, of course," and drop it, but sometimes they seemed disappointed to not get the story. I was always amazed that people didn't understand what they were asking me to do. They might as well have said, "Oh, please eviscerate yourself, right now, to pass the time for me."

———

I returned from Mexico tanned, if not healed. Still, getting away from home was helpful. I had distracted myself by shopping for chocolate and learning how to make the hot beverage many Mexicans drink, melting squares of chocolate with cinnamon, sugar, and vanilla beaten into hot milk. And I had created a new adventure, deliberately getting myself lost so I could test my rusty Spanish to ask directions.

Back home again, I returned to work, bringing souvenir silver bangles for my staff, but found that I couldn't think about anything but Becca's death. I went into my co-workers' offices to cry and get hugs and support. I apologized to my staff for not being able to provide the leadership they deserved. I had changed; life had changed; everything was different, and I no longer knew how to live, and to be.

Finally, I realized that I could not work anymore, and I took a medical leave of absence.

Sixteen

Nick, who had hurt me the most, now stayed and helped me, finding excuses to be with me by giving me what I needed—help around the house, companionship, someone to cry to, trips to the shopping mall, meatloaf dinners, and sex, the drug that was free and legal and brought temporary oblivion. He took me to place flowers on Becca's grave, and one day, understanding my need, he lay down on her grave and opened his arms to me. I had wanted to lie down beside Becca for months, but had been afraid it would mean I had lost my mind. But I lay down next to him and he held me while I wept, remembering how I had lain beside her when she was a baby.

I was torn between my anger at him and my need to be taken care of, and often wasn't kind to him. On the day I decided to tell him that he must stop coming, that I would no longer let him in, even if he used the "may I please use your bathroom" ploy, he showed up with cans of paint, rollers, brushes, and his tool box, and insisted on transforming my kitchen cupboards the way I had mentioned months earlier I wanted. It was a blistering hot day in August, the temperature over 100 degrees, and intensely humid. He stripped off his shirt and started to remove the hinges from the cabinet doors. I tried to stop him, but he was determined. He would say he did it because he loved me enough to do it. Looking back, I'd say it was true that he loved me, but he was also desperate to not lose me. Everything he did for me kept me in touch with my own neediness, and feelings of gratitude and obligation.

One evening he said, "We need to have a talk."

I was frightened about what he was going to say.

"You've been bashing me since Becca died," he said in a low voice, "and I understand why. But I can't take it anymore. I need to look for work and I can't do it feeling beat up."

"Oh, thank God!" I blurted out. "I was afraid you were going to break up with me!"

I hadn't realized how much I needed his presence in my life. I wasn't ready to lose him. Even when we were not engaged in a sexual act, the heat of our feelings for each other was undeniable and, when we were together, a comfort.

I stopped punishing him.

———

I went back to work late in the fall, only to learn that my position had been eliminated. The change was a violation of the company's published policy on medical leaves of absence, but I didn't have any fight left in me. Luckily, I was eligible for unemployment compensation, and free to go home, purge the stress of that job from my system, and look for something better.

———

As Thanksgiving approached, I began to dread the holidays without Becca. My friends Pat and Jack visited and offered me another opportunity to get away. They were living in Tokyo. "Stay with us," Pat said. "There's no Thanksgiving in Japan to remind you."

"I'd be terrible company," I told them. "I'd be crying all the time."

Pat and Jack had known Becca since she was two. Their daughters and mine had been best friends, and our families had done almost everything together. "We'll cry with you," Pat said, and I embraced them both and gratefully accepted their loving invitation. I would be their guest while I was there, and my trusty charge cards would absorb the airfare.

I was doing what many people do in times of grief—I was running. Running away, running anywhere, trying to escape the pain of Becca's death and my confusion about the relationship with Nick, as if the truth could not follow me. First Mexico, now Japan, the farthest away I could possibly get.

They met me at the airport in Tokyo and brought me back to their home, and for the next two weeks took me around Tokyo and to Nikko and Hakkoni, and every evening to a different restaurant, serving different kinds of food. I tasted yakitori (Japanese shish-ka-bob) for the first time, and Korean barbeque, and one night we sent out for a pizza, Japanese style. It came with corn on it because, Jack explained, the Japanese thought of pizza as an American dish and corn as quintessentially American.

I shopped. Using my charge cards, adding to my steeply climbing debt, I bought carvings and wooden vases and clothing to bring home, a *happi* coat for my father, a silk blouse for my mother, a kimono for Sasha. As we piled into a taxi, juggling bundles, outside a gift shop on the top of a mountain with a breathtaking view, swarming with happy-looking, picture-taking tourists, I burst into tears. "I'm buying things for everyone except Becca," I wept, missing her even there, on the other side of the world.

At the shrine at Nikko I saw a large bank of little wooden drawers, hundreds of them, and asked what they were. "They each hold a fortune," Pat explained. "Choose one drawer, and your fortune will be inside it."

I took my time examining the drawer fronts, scanning across the rows and up and down, noting the gouges and gnarls in the aged wood, the intricacies of the wood grain, the glint of sunlight on the brass drawer knobs, wondering which drawer held my fortune, and finally chose the one that seemed to call to me.

A scroll of thin white rice paper was inside. I slid it out, closed the drawer, and held my breath as I unrolled my fortune.

It was printed in Japanese. Of course! I had forgotten that it would be. None of us, Pat, Jack, nor I, could read Japanese. I tucked the fortune paper into my purse to carry around until I could find someone who could read Japanese and speak English well enough to translate it for me.

The following week Pat's friend Kazuko translated my fortune for me: "Do not travel in search of love," it read. "Stay home and it will find you." I prayed it was true.

In a market in the Shinjuku section of Tokyo I bought sake cups decorated with erotic illustrations, for Nick. Even ten thousand miles away, even after his betrayal, I was still tied to him, hooked on what he gave me.

Nick met me at the airport in Boston and drove me home, and refused to accept the cups. I was confused and hurt, but couldn't imagine that maybe he was seeing other women and didn't want any visible traces of my presence in his home. He had never let me keep any of my things at his apartment, claiming "no space for any more stuff." He was saying that again, although it was absurd, the cups were so tiny I had carried them in my purse, wrapped in tissue, all the way from Tokyo.

Still I believed him. I suppose I just didn't want to know the truth. The only men I had known before Nick were my father and brother, my high school and college boyfriends, and my husband, all of them monogamous and honest men. I had never known a Don Juan, a womanizer, and I didn't think such men really existed. It wasn't until years later, when I was finally free of my addiction to him, that I could look back and understand it.

Seventeen

I saw Grady at least once a week, sometimes more, and called her on the phone when I couldn't stop crying. She was the only person I could bare my grief to openly and honestly. She suggested I was ready to be in a bereavement group for added support. The most obvious one to turn to was Compassionate Friends, a national organization for bereaved parents. The local group was very large, and the other parents spoke of losing young children to cancer and other deadly illnesses. They were very supportive of me, and I found comfort there. But they met only once a month, which didn't feel like enough, so I also joined a ten-week bereavement support group at a local hospice. Those people, too, were very kind to me, everyone understanding the pain we all felt, although no one else there had lost a child or experienced a sudden, violent loss. I still needed more—more shared experience, more meetings, more bonding with others who felt as I did. I continued attending both groups and looking around for more support.

Somehow I learned of a small group for survivors of homicide victims, and I scheduled an intake interview. By then, Becca had been dead for about a year, the time when people had said I'd be "over it," but I wasn't. At the interview I asked Scott, the therapist who led the group, "Am I crazy?"

"No," he said quietly but emphatically. "It takes much, much longer to recover from what you've lost, what you've been through, than people who haven't gone through it understand. You're just where anyone would be. You'll meet people in the group for whom it has been longer, and they'll tell you how much it still hurts. But they can help you."

———

At the beginning of every meeting Scott said to us, "I cannot possibly know the depths of your great pain, and I know that I'm lucky not to.

But I hope that by being here, listening, and providing this opportunity for you to support each other, I may somehow contribute to your healing." We loved him for that, and the healing I received in that group was immeasurable and changed my life. That experience and Scott's example made me want to become a therapist like Grady, and like him.

People in the group were at various stages in their journey of healing, depending on the violence of their loss, how long ago it had happened, and what else in their lives had complicated it. Those for whom the loss still felt raw talked about the constant feeling of having had their hearts pulled out by the roots. Many of us were struggling to get out of bed each day, some of us weren't always able to do even that, and our minds were constantly assaulted by terrible questions: Did this really happen? How could it happen to my child? To us? Was it my fault? Is God punishing me? Will I always hurt this much? How will I get through the rest of my life? Is this a dream, a nightmare, and when can I wake up?

Years later, when I thanked Scott and told him that I admired his work with bereavement, he said, "Thanks, Sam, but that wasn't about bereavement. It was about trauma."

That was when I realized why I had felt as though the sky had fallen and crushed me into fragments. I had been blindsided, assaulted by my relentless visions of how Becca had died, of her violent departure from me, and from life. Trauma was the reason my brain had shut down and taken off into the realm of perpetual darkness and fear.

———————

As some friends continued to fall away, loyal friends pulled in closer. Marilyn and Mike checked in on me and invited me to join them for easy things—a walk around the pond, a pizza and a movie on DVD, a dinner at their home. It may have been a coincidence, but I noticed that the people who stayed with me were either people with children or people who had lost someone they had loved very much. Those who didn't know the pain of such a loss and couldn't imagine it, broke dates, stopped calling, and got on with their busy lives, adding to my loss.

I slept poorly, my fits of dozing increasingly invaded by dreams, all of them about Becca. In every dream, she was a tiny girl of five, wearing the too-big green raincoat she had worn then, and in every dream she said good-bye and cheerfully went away, too young to understand that it was forever, and I woke up crying.

During the day my body ached with fatigue and my mind felt foggy from months of sleep deprivation. My abdomen hurt most of all. Eventually I consulted a doctor who identified growths on one ovary that could be malignant. People had told me that bereaved mothers were at high risk for serious illness, most notably cancer. My body had begun to register the collective emotional trauma to my mind—the years of caring for and worrying about my family, the loss of my marriage and our family home, Nick's duplicity, and now especially the loss of Becca, my baby—and illness was emerging where motherhood arises, in my reproductive organs. So one year after Becca's death I had major surgery, and the growths, which were revealed to be precancerous, were removed in time.

Being ill or convalescing at home as a single person living alone is another one of those ordeals people can't imagine unless they have done it or helped someone in that situation. No one warned me that when I returned home there would be things I would need—pain medication, extra pillows, small high-protein meals, dressings and medications for the incision—that I would be unable to shop for myself.

The first challenge to the patient living alone is getting the medicine prescribed upon discharge. Marilyn had taken me to the hospital and waited in the family waiting room for the surgeon to come out and report how the operation had gone, and Mike brought me home five days later. He generously offered to run my drugstore and supermarket errands, and I accepted, but asking people to take care of me did not come easily. I struggled to do it alone until I found myself, one day, lying on the floor of my bedroom, because I had become light-headed and fallen. I felt so alone at that moment, wedged between the bed and the wall, seeing only the tan flecks of tweed in the carpeting, with no one to call out to. I lay there and cried until the pain of the fall and my self-pity receded and I could summon the energy to pull myself up onto the bed. Once safely back there, I picked up the phone and called my friend Louise, who loved to nurture. "I need help," I told her, and just those three magic words were all she needed to hear. She came over and helped me figure out that I was hungry and needed to keep snacks in my bedroom, which was separated from the kitchen by a flight of stairs I couldn't negotiate yet. She set up a "feeding station" beside my bed and stocked it with fruit, crackers, cheese, and peanut butter, all things that could keep well and be eaten at room temperature.

Still feeling frustrated and sorry for myself, I called Marilyn the next morning. Mike answered the phone. "You said you'd help me when I got home from the hospital," I tearfully accused him, "but you're not."

"Just tell me what you want," he said, "and I'll do it."

"I need breakfast in the morning," I sniffled, "and I can't get to the kitchen because I can't do stairs yet."

The next day, and every day until I was able to use the stairs, he stopped in on his way to work, cooked some oatmeal, and brought it to me on a tray with fruit and a pitcher of milk. Marilyn would call me later in the day to offer to do an errand, or to share some of their dinner. At the same time that I was learning how tenuous some friendships could be, I was also learning how deep friendship could run, and—equally important—that I could ask for the help I needed.

————

I asked Grady for a referral to a psychiatrist to prescribe medication to stop my constant weeping.

The psychiatrist asked me back to her office for several visits, listened closely to what I had experienced—the long string of pain and disappointment and losses that stretched back for years—and told me my response to what had happened was normal. "I don't want to stop your tears," she said. "I want you to go home and cry a whole lot more."

Ironically, I felt better hearing this. So I was not crazy! I was merely heartbroken, beaten, battered and exhausted from my life, my anger, my losses, and painful longings for Becca that were, taken together, just normal, accumulated, devastating grief.

So I went home and dreamed the excruciating dreams of Becca, and watched the horrible movie in my mind, and wept a whole lot more.

Eighteen

I have always drawn great comfort and inspiration from books, but now found myself, mysteriously and frustratingly, unable to read. My mind would not take in words from a page, and every time I attempted to read a book, I forgot the beginning of a sentence by the time I reached its end. But I kept trying, combing the libraries and stores for books that would help me understand what I was going through and how to live with the emotional pain that had begun to attack my body.

Then I discovered a book that would set the course for my recovery. It was *Coming Back* by Dr. Ann Kaiser Stearns, a psychologist and author of many books, and was filled with stories of people who had weathered crises and lists of things that helped them. Try as I did, I still couldn't read the whole book, or even a chapter. I went through the pages hoping that something would stick to my brain, and finally, in the last chapter, I found one paragraph that coalesced from letters to words to concepts, and entered my brain as thoughts, ideas, something I could use.

Dr. Stearns cited a research study by the International Committee for the Study of Victimization that showed that trauma survivors ultimately fall into three categories of roughly equal size: those who are crushed by their misfortune and never recover, those who succeed in regaining their previous level of functioning, and those who grow from the experience and feel stronger and capable of achieving more than they had before the traumatic event.

The first group was not news to me. A would-be well-wisher at Becca's funeral had held my hand and told me, "I have a friend who lost her daughter years ago. She never got over it." I was frightened by what I'm sure she meant as another way of saying, "I understand your pain is immense," but reached my ears instead as, "You'll always feel as terrible as you do now."

I knew what that looked like. A former neighbor became darkly and permanently morose after his daughter died. Children in the neighborhood who once loved the man were now afraid of him because he waved his cane to shoo them out of his way, snarling and spewing his anger.

I knew I didn't want to go through life feeling like that. Returning to my previous level of functioning would be wonderful, but how much better to honor Becca's memory by accomplishing something as a tribute to her! Up to this point all I had been aware of was the waste of her shortened life and the pain of the many people who loved her. Maybe I could use the pain as a foundation to build on, to keep it from being wasted. How, I needed to know, did one get into that third category of those who grow from tragedy, trauma, and loss?

The chapter contained three full pages of techniques that fostered healing, thirty-eight suggestions in all. I tried to read them, but the words separated again into meaningless letters. I couldn't read any more.

When I came back to the book the next day, I looked at the long list again and again. I still couldn't absorb it all. Only three elements emerged and penetrated my fogged brain to any degree. As best as I could decipher, I needed support from other people, I needed to believe in something beyond the material dimension, and I needed a personal goal.

That was all my mind could accommodate. I hoped that if I could have these three things in my life, they could serve as ingredients of a recipe to restore positive meaning to my shattered life. I wanted this as much as I had wanted to be mother to my girls. My job as Becca's mother was not over, and I was not quitting—not now, when I could see a possible way out of the darkness, and a way to make her life and her death count for more.

——— ———

I inventoried my life for the three ingredients on my list. I had support from Grady, my close friends, and the homicide support group. But I lacked a spiritual or religious belief, a faith in something larger than myself. I also lacked a personal goal. I decided to devote myself to finding a spiritual belief and a personal goal, to position myself in that third category of survivors.

——— ———

The God of my childhood sat behind a large, glass-topped mahogany desk in downtown heaven. It was like my father's desk in his law office downtown, but much, much larger. God, like my father, may have had snapshots of his children and newspaper clippings describing his achievements beneath the glass. God's skin was white, like mine, as was his shoulder-length hair and the beard that extended to just below his waist. He wore a white robe tied at the waist with a rope. I knew he watched me constantly and punished me when I was bad, because if I accidentally hurt myself, maybe whacked my elbow against a corner of the kitchen table right after I had "talked back" to my mother, she would say, "See? God punished you." It happened with maddening reliability.

I took this vision of God-As-Larger-Than-Life-Parent with me all the way to college, where in late-night discussions in the dorm, my friends and I agreed that God was a placebo, an illusory crutch for needy people. We did not see ourselves as needy, which was an unpopular thing to be, so as a group we threw away our crutches and turned instead to the study of Greek and Oriental philosophers—Plato, Socrates, Lao Tzu—whom we found more credible, and the Existentialists—Gide, Sartre—not even noticing that they were all men, since in the '50s, almost everything considered important seemed to be understood and taught by men. My personal favorites were Lao Tzu, the Chinese philosopher behind the teachings of the *Tau Te Ching*, and Decartes, the pragmatist, who said, "*Cogito ergo sum*," which has been translated variously to, "I think, therefore I am," or "I think, which proves that I exist." I liked the universalism of the Tau and the simplicity of pragmatism, but the lure, for me, was actually the excitement of exploring unfamiliar cultures and beliefs, dabbling in other languages, seeing reality from new perspectives.

My confirmation as an atheist took place at 35,000 feet, the first time I flew in a jet, when I was nineteen and saw what was really above the clouds. I had never seen such stark, pure, far-reaching beauty. If there was a God, I concluded, I could readily see how this is where He would choose to live. But I didn't see Him there, and I took that as proof of his nonexistence.

After college I felt no need for religion or philosophy. Finding a job, an apartment, and then a husband, all seemed to occur outside of any belief system other than, "It's time." When it was time to marry, I did. When it was time to have children, we did. I don't recall ever turning to God. We believed in ourselves as the source of all that we needed. I had felt no need for a belief in, or a relationship with, God.

But I was in my fifties now, and Becca was gone, and I needed to believe and have faith that somehow I could not only live with the loss of her, but become stronger, more alive, because of it. I would achieve this, and identify a worthy goal. I didn't wonder whether or how I could do it, I simply decided I would.

I had always felt driven to take on challenges and complete them well. As a child growing up I saw every school assignment, every extracurricular activity, as an opportunity to make my parents proud of me, to deserve their love. This had evolved into my persona of The Girl Who Gets Things Done.

Moreover, about eight years earlier I had taken one of the most influential courses I had ever been exposed to, called DMA, for Dimensional Mind Approach, developed and taught by Robert Fritz, a brilliant organizational consultant and writer. To those of us who took the course, it became known as "the most wonderful course with the most awful name," because the name didn't hint at the greatness of what Mr. Fritz was teaching. The subtitle of his subsequent book, *Path of Least Resistance: Learning to Become the Creative Force in Your Own Life*, was more to the point. The course taught that whatever we want in life, we can manifest, by intending it strongly and aiming for it truly.

How I came to take the course was a lesson in itself. A friend had given my contact information to the program office, and they called to invite me to sign up.

The tuition sounded steep to me, so I declined, telling the caller that the price was out of my reach.

"Would you like to take the course if you had the money?" she asked, and I admitted I would.

"I suggest, then," she said, "that you register with us now, and if you really want, and intend, to take the course, the money will become available to you. If it doesn't, there will be no penalty for canceling."

That seemed far-fetched, but I figured if it worked, if it could make money appear, then this was a course I'd be interested in taking.

I registered over the phone, and before she signed off the caller said, "Now remember, you're planning to take the course on these dates, and you are expecting the money to show up. That's all you have to do."

About two weeks later I received a surprise in the mail, a check for a little more than the amount of the tuition, from a forgotten bank account that had been closed because of its inactivity. The money was a total windfall, and I took it as a sign that I should take the course.

Using the techniques of self-hypnosis and visualization I learned from DMA, I had accomplished everything that had been hanging over me, uncompleted, at home and at work. I was able to fit more into every day, take the children to their appointments, make some of their clothes, keep up with the house, write, and make it to my job.

We had been strongly warned in the course that it would be impossible to cause anyone else to behave in a certain way, and that it would be unethical to try. So while I had accomplished what I wanted for myself, I had been unable to make Paul act according to my choices. I could set goals for myself, and that's all.

Now, with Becca gone and my life stretched out ahead of me with only the pain guaranteed, I needed to pull in every resource I had to identify and accomplish my own goals. I simply had to intend to, and pursue my intention. I didn't know how I would do it, and I never gave a thought to what it might cost me

.

Nineteen

In winter a pocket-size magazine began to arrive regularly in the mail. The first time it came I gave it only a glance and concluded that it was a religious tract. I wasn't interested. I discarded it with the rest of the unsolicited mail.

A month later, another issue arrived and this time I noticed the title before throwing it out: *Daily Word*. When a third one came a month later, I flipped through it and saw that there was an uplifting message for each day of the month. I read a few and found them more poetic and spiritual than religious, although each page also bore a line from the Old or New Testament. When the fourth issue came in the mail, curiosity motivated me to put it on my nightstand to look through during the hour before turning out the light, my habitual reading time.

I found the daily readings inspiring, gentle, drawn from many faiths, and more about concepts of love, hope, strength, and living to the best of one's ability than about adoration of a supreme being. The magazine came from a spiritual learning center with Christian roots, but widened to embrace principles common to most faiths. Each day's reading had a heading (for example, "Inner Peace") and then a few paragraphs about the subject, including affirmations, such as, "When I shift my focus and return to center, I am reminded of the deep peace within." Each page, for each day, had a different theme, such as faith, grace, joy, or kindness.

I became a devotee of the booklet and began a morning ritual of reading the daily message.

———————

I brought a copy with me when I met Judith for a walk on the beach. "I want to show you something," I said, pulling it out of my pocket as we walked. "I think someone may have given me a subscription to this little magazine, and it's wonderful."

"Sam," she said, as soon as she saw it, "that was me. I sent you a gift subscription."

"Oh," I said. "How wonderful! Thank you, I love it. I must have thrown out the card with the other mail."

"I've been reading it for years," she said, "and I thought you would like it. I sent gift subscriptions at Christmas to all my close friends."

That booklet, which I still subscribe to and read today, was where I began to find meaning, something to believe in, the second ingredient in the "category three" recipe for survival and growth. I now had a form of prayer that felt right to me: reading the message for each day, contemplating it, and going into the day feeling connected to something larger than myself. I was connected to the thoughts and values of all the people who read the booklet, starting with my wonderful, generous friend Judith.

Twenty

I needed to get back to work and earn a living, but I was still emotionally fragile, afraid of everything, and unable to focus on anything or think quickly. I asked Marilyn and Mike for advice, and Mike assured me he really needed someone to work part-time in the business office of his factory, opening mail, answering the phone, keeping records. He gave me my choice of hours and days, and I slowly made my way back to the routine of work, initially for three afternoons a week, until I felt able to work more hours and more days.

Every time I drove to work I had to pass a giant billboard with a picture of a crashed automobile. The public education message printed above it read, "Seat belts save lives." I hated that billboard—Becca had probably not been wearing her seat belt—and I believed I saw a body trapped in the wreckage of the car. I asked people at the factory who drove by that sign whether I was imagining the body in the car. They didn't see it. Apparently I was picturing her death in my mind.

I was very afraid, and would be for a long time, to drive past the scene of automobile accidents, or to travel the highway on which she had been killed. Scott, the leader of the homicide support group, had been right—this business of recovery took a long time. I wondered whether I would ever feel normal—regain my sense of direction and the ability to think clearly, remember telephone numbers, calculate a restaurant tip in my head, get a good night's sleep and wake up in the morning not crying—or ever experience joy again.

I worked part-time for more than a year before I finally felt ready to return to full-time work, and in the spring of 1990, two years after Becca's death, I started sending out resumes. I pulled myself together and went to job interviews. Being back in the job market felt strange, because having been through something life-changing, I felt like a different person from the woman I had been. I now carried an invisible weight of grief that I kept hidden. I felt lucky when I was hired by a medical software company to do customer support, combining my computer skills with my background in hospital work.

———————

I still needed that third element of Category Three in the recovery protocol, a personal goal. I hated to get out of bed mornings because I saw nothing to live for, except Sasha. I also knew that if I was going to find any happiness in my life, it would have to be in my work.

I remembered how my father's love of his work had kept him active and happy. When I was a child I saw him leave for work eagerly every morning, dressed up in his best suit and tie, toting his important leather briefcase. I had watched him back the car out of the rented garage two houses away and return hours later after his mysterious day away, apparently still happy.

I also saw my mother stuck at home without a car, doing housework and tired much of the time from the demands of her traditional role. Having noted that the world seemed to be half male and half female, and not realizing that the die had already been cast, I fervently wished that I would grow up to be a man, so I could be the one to leave the house and do work that would invigorate me and make me happy. Now in his eighties, my dad was still practicing law and leaving the house in the same way every day, looking forward to his workday. I needed that, to wake up with something to look forward to every day—to want to get out of bed, and to live—and it would have to be my work.

I'd always wanted to be a healer, had chosen pre-med as one of my majors in college, aspiring to psychiatry as a specialty. But when it came time to apply to medical schools, my parents couldn't afford to send me, and there were no student loans in those days. So with my dual degree in pre-med and chemistry I had gone to work instead as a research biochemist, and soon afterward I met Paul. I left research to become a teacher for a brief time, and then a stay-at-home mom. But what I was looking for now was not a job, but a calling. I needed work I would love, that would be meaningful to me, that would somehow allow me to use all of who I am.

———————

I still longed for the pain in my heart to go away, and was still looking for her. She was nowhere; and yet she was everywhere.

86

In a cruiser with blue lights flashing, a state police officer drove me to the spot where it had happened. He waited above on the road as I made my way down the steep embankment, clutching a bouquet of roses in one arm and using the other to grab at branches and lean against boulders, to maintain my balance. Down in the gully, far below the roar of the mid-day traffic, I cast about for the spot where she may have landed.

One flat stretch of grass seemed to say to me, "Over here, Mom. This is where I died."

I lay the flowers on the spot and stood back. *Becca*, I said silently, *I'm so sorry this happened to you. May you be at peace. May nothing ever hurt you again.*

I hoped this was where my heart could finally come to rest, with her.

I expanded my morning ritual by following my reading of *Daily Word* with a period of sitting quietly with my thoughts about a Higher Power, a Higher Purpose, a reason for my life. I practiced talking to God, feeling foolish at first, but soon finding hope and comfort in the practice. I slowly came to believe that there could be a Divine purpose in work, a reason that transcended merely earning a living in order to pay the mortgage and buy the groceries and take an occasional vacation. I wanted meaning, and I had been looking hard at my skills and things that brought me joy. I love words, I love people, I have natural empathy—there must be work that I was meant to be doing, what Buddhists call Right Livelihood, which does more than earn money for stockholders, which contributes in some way to the needs of those who want or need a better quality of life.

I consulted a vocational psychologist who met me in the pine-paneled basement office in his home. Howard interviewed me, administered several written and oral tests, and had me write my autobiography. By our third meeting he had enough information to address the question of what my right work might be.

"Whatever you do, Sam," he said, "don't go to work in the insurance business."

I was shocked. The company I had left when Becca died was a medical insurance company, and I was now being courted by a life insurance company and considering taking a position there. "Why not?"

"Because you don't love money enough," he said. "In fact, you don't seem to care much about money at all. Business is about making money, that has to drive you if you're going to succeed."

"Years ago I had a piano tuning business," I reminded him, "and it was a great success."

"That's because you love music and musicians; that's why your business was so successful. You need to be among people you enjoy, and you're motivated by your desire to help others."

I remembered that when I did temporary office work I had spent two weeks as a front desk receptionist, giving people directions. I had loved when people said "Thank you!" with such obvious appreciation when I told them to take the elevator to the third floor and turn left getting off. I had enjoyed feeling helpful. *Maybe my calling is to be a receptionist*, I had thought. I had been offered the position permanently and would have accepted it but the salary was too low to support my family of four.

In the back of my mind for so many years was the unspoken dream that I ventured to give voice to now. "Howard," I said hesitantly, "do you think . . . I've always wondered if I could . . . would I make a good psychotherapist, do you think?"

"Sam," he said without any hesitation, "you would be a natural. You'd be good at it, and it's a perfect profession for you. It matches your skills and your values. It doesn't pay that well, but that won't matter to you. If that's what you'd like to do, I say go for it!"

Being a psychotherapist, doing the work I had seen Grady and Scott do, seemed like the work that I, *the woman who listens*, had been born to do. I was thrilled at the prospect.

My next step was to research the possibilities. "Psychotherapist" is a generic term, and can refer to anyone who claims to be one. But to be licensed to practice, a person needs to be trained and credentialed in a recognized discipline. My friend Alice and I attended a conference at which representatives from the fields of psychiatry, psychology, clinical social work, education, nursing, and counseling spoke about their professions—the required education and qualifications, the earning opportunities, the status of each discipline in various work environments. I interviewed psychotherapists I knew socially, got as much advice and information as I could, and found that for me, all arrows pointed to clinical social work. Alice made a different choice, to pursue a doctorate in psychology. Both choices would qualify us to apply for licensure as psychotherapists.

Before entering treatment with Grady I hadn't known what social workers do. I admired and envied her skills and what she could accomplish with them. Then, in the homicide support group, I had met Scott, also a clinical social worker, and my attraction to the field increased. I questioned all the clinical social workers practicing as psychotherapists that I could, and they unanimously expressed satisfaction with their work. I was fifty-two. I could hope to complete the graduate education and training for the license to practice independently in four to five years, whereas medicine or psychology would take longer, and I didn't need that breadth of education, since I knew that therapy—not medical management, and not research—was what I wanted to do.

I explored the accredited graduate schools of social work within commuting distance and found only one program that I could attend part-time while I continued to work full-time. That had been Howard's idea, too. "Work and go to school simultaneously until you need to make your choice. By then you will have enough information to know whether you want to pursue social work full-time or let it go, and you'll already have a job you can stay with. Either way, you win, because the choice will be yours."

That had been Grady's advice, too, time and again, when she had said, "When you have enough information, your choice will be clear."

Boston University's Graduate School of Social Work had an off-campus program that met weekends throughout the year for three years, located close to my parents' house. I could continue working full-time and also attend school, staying with my parents on the weekends. BU had a great reputation and was respected everywhere. I applied for admission to the class beginning in September 1990.

Part III

Climbing

Twenty-one

"I could use a break," I told Joseph, my friend in Washington, DC, "and I've always wanted to see the cherry blossoms. Are they in bloom?"

"They're just opening," he said. "This weekend would be the best time."

He met me at the airport and gave me a tour of the city. I got to see the cherry blossoms, already dropping petals on the grass beneath, and went to the Smithsonian to see the African exhibits. The best day of the weekend was Sunday, when we went to Mount Vernon and an elegant colonial-style restaurant, where we dined on fine food in a setting that felt two hundred years old. Afterward, as we toured the grounds of George Washington's home on the Potomac, snow began to fall. I looked up and saw snowflakes landing lightly on the flowering redbud trees, and the juxtaposition of cold whiteness and magenta blossoms moved me to gasp in appreciation and burn the image into my mind, so that I remember it still. Snow on flowers. I'm told that the Japanese have long held those to be two of the three most beautiful things in nature. The third is the moon.

That night we sipped tea, each leaning on a cushioned arm of the long sofa in Joseph's living room, facing each other, legs stretched out before us, and we talked, as we had for years—about our marriages, divorces, friendships, life, and death. I wept for Becca, telling Joseph how hard I found life since she was gone, and then suddenly came to my senses and stopped.

"Oh, Joseph," I said, "Forgive me. I forgot. You don't have children. But which is worse do you think, losing a child, or never having had one?"

"All I can tell you, Sam," he said, "is this: I envy you."

He envied me. The realization hit me, that I did not hold a monopoly on suffering. I didn't even have the saddest life. I could finally see that other people had pain, too.

Joseph and I spoke on the phone many times before he died a few years later from lung cancer, and he often told me that he fondly remembered the beauty of that day, when we had seen snow on the blossoming redbud. That was the day I had begun to see beauty again and to let it in, where it could nurture me and help me heal.

My application to BU was denied. At first I was incredulous, and then sad, but both feelings quickly mutated to anger, and then desperation. This was my only chance! I phoned the office of the Dean of Admissions.

"I'd like to know why I was rejected, and whether I can do anything to change it," I said.

The Dean looked up my file. "You were rejected because you have no social work background, your college grades were too low, and your degree isn't in liberal arts."

"How do I appeal the decision?" I asked.

"You would have to write a letter to the Dean of the School of Social Work," she said.

I spent the next few days in a frenzy of writing and ended up with a three-page single-spaced letter that pointed out that my undergraduate grades were more than thirty years old, that I had spent those thirty-plus years doing what social workers do—community work, child care, problem solving, managing family dynamics and illnesses—and that no twenty-two-year-old recent college graduate in liberal arts could possibly have a broader, fuller background than life and travel had given me. My letter had an edge of anger and a hint of accusation, but I had nothing to lose. I gave it everything I had, typed and printed it, and mailed it.

The secretary to the Dean of the School of Social Work called in a few days and told me the Dean would like to meet with me.

I treated the appointment as the most important interview of my life. I asked Alice to help me pick out what to wear. I had thought a business suit would convey professionalism and achievement.

"No," she said, "this isn't about a manager's position. You want to look like a social worker. Wear something soft."

We went through my closet and chose a full cranberry-red challis skirt with a matching blouse, gold stud earrings and a delicate, short, gold chain necklace, and shoes with low heels.

"There," she said, "now you look like a dressed-up social worker."

I planned what I would say, made notes on small file cards, and retrieved newspaper stories about my father that read, "Dean of the Bar Practicing Law for Fifty-five Years." When I arrived at the Dean's office I asked his secretary how much time he had allocated for our appointment.

"One hour," she told me.

I calculated how best to use that hour. I'd ask my questions in the first few minutes, sell myself for the next half hour or so, and leave time for his questions at the end.

Dean Hubie Jones was a prominent personality in Boston, a regular on a televised Sunday morning panel discussion of public affairs, an eloquent speaker, and an advocate for the rights of the disenfranchised and minorities. He welcomed me warmly and invited me to sit at the small, round table in his office, away from his desk.

I launched into my pitch. "What were the reasons I was denied admission?" I asked, hoping I sounded reasonable, pleasant, and intelligent. "What were the objections?"

"Actually," he said, "your application was read twice, which we don't usually do. But both times, the committee felt that your background contained nothing to indicate experience or motivation in the field of social work." He stopped.

I took over and talked for the next thirty minutes. I told him about raising my children and organizing activities for them and their friends; overseeing their safety, nutritional, medical, and developmental needs; serving at their school as a library aide, a Brownie troop meeting leader, and a writing-workshop teacher; serving on local political committees and organizing town activities; and advocating for my parents in their old age and for my husband throughout his long period of mental illness.

I pulled out the newspaper clippings about my father, photographed at his desk, flashing an obviously self-satisfied smile. "This is my father," I said. "He's eighty-three years old and he's still practicing law, going to court every day, and he's healthy and in good spirits. He loves his work. I've watched him go to work all my life, and seen the energy and fulfillment it has given him, and it's what I want for myself, a profession that makes me want to go to work, that I can be proud of, that will keep me active and healthy at least into my eighties, too."

Dean Jones seemed fascinated by the newspaper clippings. He was in his fifties, like me, and wanted to know more about my father and his work, and enjoyed the stories I had to tell.

At some point I glanced at my watch and saw that we were almost at the forty-five minute mark in our hour. "Please tell me what reservations you still have about me, so that I can address them," I said.

"Well," he said, ruminating briefly, "you're in the program—"

"I *am?*" I interrupted, too amazed and excited to contain myself.

"Yes," he said, "you are, and I have no reservations whatsoever about you. You'll do just fine."

"Thank you, thank you," I gushed, and the tone of our meeting immediately changed to friendly chatting about my father and mutual acquaintances. He wished me luck and I promised we'd meet and talk again soon.

My old life had ended with Becca's death in 1988, and my new life was beginning now, in 1990. That evening Sasha and I went out for dinner to celebrate and we called my parents, she to tell them she had been admitted to a new college that day, and I to tell them I was going to graduate school.

Dean Hubie Jones and I became friends at school and he was right, I did just fine.

On a glorious, warm, sunny day in August my friend Carol and I drove to Point Judith in Rhode Island. The day was picture perfect, with a light salt breeze drifting in over the water, making the air soft and cool. As we tooled along with the top down, sometimes singing along with the music on the radio, I felt my heart overflowing with something warm and new, yet familiar. "If anyone had told me after Becca's death that I would ever feel joy again," I said, "I wouldn't have believed it. But at this moment, I feel actual joy."

It was only the first time. Joy began to come increasingly often, until it eventually occupied more of my life than did pain and sadness. That would take years, but learning that day that joy could happen again was a stunning gift.

Twenty-two

At the end of the summer Alice and I threw a party for our neighbors, one last fling before we both burrowed into our studies for the long haul. I was showered with warm good-bye-and-good-lucks, and a few smaller parties in the neighborhood were thrown for me in the following days.

For the next thirty-three months, my weekdays consisted of going to work every day, and coming home to study and write term papers every night. I left work early on Fridays and drove to school, and when class ended late at night I drove to my parents' house to sleep. In the morning, after an early breakfast with them, I went back to school for the Saturday class, and arrived back at my own house late that day, exhausted. Sundays were for washing a week's worth of dishes, doing laundry, shopping for groceries, and getting to bed early enough to be able to repeat it all the next week. It was a grueling pace, but I was driven, focused on my goal of becoming a psychotherapist, an essential ingredient in the Recipe to make my life positive. It made getting up every morning not only possible but worthwhile again. I had to imbue Becca's death with meaning, doing what had characterized her and her life—helping others.

At one of our first class meetings we were each asked to tell the other students about our professional and academic backgrounds and our reasons for being in the program. I thought about what had brought me here, and I realized I couldn't talk about that without crying. When it came my turn to speak, I knew this was my chance to ask for what I needed.

"We're going to be together for the next three years," I said, as I stood and faced them, "and I'd like to make a request of you all. Two years ago, my daughter was killed . . . " Here my voice broke and the tears began. I forged ahead, weeping openly. "My daughter Rebecca,

Becca for short, was a very gentle, caring, compassionate young woman. I want to carry on her purpose of comforting and supporting others, and a large part of my reason for entering this field is to help people dealing with loss and trauma. I want to make bereavement and trauma my clinical specialties. But I know that in order to do it, I'm going to have to be able to talk about this, about my daughter, without crying. If you would please indulge me over the time we are in this program together, and tolerate my tears, I believe it will help me reach a point where I can talk about it, think about it, work with it, without crying. Allowing me to talk about it and cry will be how you can support me, and I'd really appreciate it."

I could tell from their upturned faces and sympathetic eyes that they were with me, willing to support me, and I took my seat, shaking, but very grateful to have found my way to this place.

———————

In February, between courses, on a brief business trip to Florida for the software company I worked for, I took a few days to travel on my own. I took a ride in a swamp buggy, walked a boardwalk in the Everglades, and saw my first egrets and flamingos. I called friends I hadn't seen since I was a teenager and had a lovely reunion with them overlooking the waters of Tampa Bay. Before dusk on the last day, just over the bridge connecting Sanibel and Captiva Islands, I parked my rented car on a strip of gravel where dozens of cars were lined up facing the sunset. I sat on the hood of my car and watched the spectacle for which that strip of beach is famous, as the blood-red orb slowly approached the watery horizon reflecting the spreading colors. The sound of cameras clicked up and down the beach as scores of other people, in pairs and groups, "oohed" and "aahed" at the show. At that moment I felt lonely, awkward in my singleness, wishing I had someone to share it with.

A couple about my age stood in front of the car parked next to mine. She was enjoying the sunset as much as I, but he was restless and eager to leave. "C'mon," he said, opening the driver's door, "let's go. It's just a sunset."

"But it's not over," she protested.

"You've seen sunsets before," he growled, getting into the car. "Let's go."

"Can't we wait?" she pleaded. "Just a few more minutes?"

"Get in. Let's go!" he snapped, and started the engine.

As she moved away from the sunset to get into the car, her eyes caught mine and seemed to say, *I envy you, alone, doing as you please.*

I'm sorry you have to leave with him, I said silently to her with my eyes.

She turned in resignation toward the passenger door and climbed in, and they left.

Maybe I'm the lucky one, I thought.

I was gradually coming to understand that I didn't need a man to make me complete. I could travel on my own, attend a concert by myself, and buy my own perfume and jewelry, all things that would never have occurred to me as a married woman. I realized that without Paul I was still a valuable person, and without Nick I was still sexy and beautiful. I may have lost Paul's love, and had made a huge mistake in trusting Nick, but the things they had taught me were mine to keep and to build on. I also understood that romantic love was not all that mattered. The love of my daughters, parents, cousins, and friends meant more, ran deeper, and didn't stem from anyone's neurotic need.

Becca had stated it very well years earlier when she was about fifteen and we were leaving a family celebration together. Grandparents, aunts and uncles, cousins—first, second, and once removed—the whole, extended family had been there.

"I just realized something about family," she told me, when we settled into the car for the ride home. "They all love me. I don't have to do anything, I just show up, and they love me!"

Now I was learning this for myself. Although I had grown up thinking I had to earn love, I finally realized there was love I already had, and always would. More important was the understanding that I could love myself. Weeks earlier I had said to Grady, "I have this feeling of being in love, but I look around and there's nobody else here, nobody I'm in love with, so I'm thinking, maybe it's me. Maybe I'm in love with me!"

She had nodded and smiled broadly at me for figuring it out.

A few days later a friend, seeing a dozen deep red long-stemmed roses in a vase on my kitchen table, said, "Oh, roses! Who loves you enough to buy you roses?"

"I do," I answered.

Twenty-three

Apart from the brief getaway to Florida, school and work consumed all my time. I stayed in touch with Sasha by phone. Nick kept calling, but I had neither the time nor the desire to see him.

My classmates represented a wide range of professional backgrounds and ages. At fifty-two I was the second oldest. Most were women, and everyone had day jobs, some in the field of social work and others, like me, in unrelated areas.

I got to be something of a joke because initially I was so unfamiliar with the vocabulary, I didn't even understand the course titles. One course was called Differential Diagnosis. The only use of "differential" I knew was the name of an automobile part. We were weeks into the course before I caught on that as clinicians called upon to diagnose, we needed skills for *differentiating* among disorders that shared some symptoms, such as panic disorder and phobias, which can look the same but have different causes and require different treatments.

The class spoke in sets of initials, such as the *DSM* (*Diagnostic and Statistical Manual*) or ADHD (Attention Deficit Hyperactivity Disorder), which were new to me, and used words like *decompensate* and *case management*, which I didn't understand. So I filled the margins of my notebook with words and acronyms I didn't know, and looked them up or asked someone privately about it after class. And every time I raised my hand to ask a question, I began with the same disclaimer, "Well, I'm not really a social worker yet, so this may sound like a stupid question . . . " and after the third time, the class laughed whenever I said it because it had become so predictable. Finally one of the professors said, very kindly and with a smile, "Sam, why don't you just skip that part and get to the question," and the class cheered.

I loved school and what I was learning, and looked forward to the weekends and the drive there. In the fall my first clinical internship would occupy two full days every week, and the time to choose between staying with my job or committing to the master's degree program was drawing close.

My choice was easy. In August I left my full-time employment and lined up several part-time, midweek jobs that would allow me to serve my internship and continue to attend school on the weekends.

———————

Before going back to school after the short August break, I spent a week at an adult camp on Casco Bay in Maine. Traveling solo can be distinctly unpleasant at places where everyone else seems to be coupled or in families or groups, so I had scouted out places where I could arrive alone and quickly feel part of a group. The camp at Ferry Beach was like that. All the guests ate meals together at long tables in the dining room, where we sang songs after clearing away our own dishes, and hung out on the porch when we weren't participating in the variety of activities available. Making new friends was expected and easy. By the end of the week I was feeling comfortable enough to sign up for the talent show on the last night. As one of the oldest people there, with my natural reserve and quiet ways, I probably appeared rather dignified and prim, an image that would enhance what I had planned for my performance.

I enlisted the help of the kitchen staff, and borrowed a long skirt from a new friend to wear with my hiking boots and to cover my rolled up jeans and the pot lids strapped to my knees.

On stage, in front of the whole camp, I invited another camper to accompany me on the banjo while I taught the audience a song.

"Now, foller me," I twanged, slapping a straw hat onto my head and shooting them a big grin, showing my blackened-out front teeth. "She'll be a'comin' 'round the mountain when she comes!" I sang, and lifted my skirt to my chin, spread my blue-jeaned knees apart, slapped the pot lids together with a loud "clang! clang!" then quickly dropped my skirt and went on to the next line.

The audience gasped collectively, and I heard a few shrieks of astonishment. They seemed not altogether sure what had happened, it had all been so fast.

I sang the second line, same as the first but a little higher, and when I raised my skirt and clanged my pot lids again, the audience broke into laughter that didn't stop. I went through the whole song, turning around to give them the backside view, and clapping and urging them to sing along. Their laughter was a constant roar. At the

101

end of the show they called for a reprise, in which the whole cast joined me.

I'd never behaved so outrageously, or had more fun, and discovering I could do that, and make other people so happy, fed me with a surge of energy I'd never known.

After the show I was too elated to slow down and go back to my bunk. A few other performers felt the same, so we drove to nearby Old Orchard Beach, with its honky-tonk boardwalk, where my still-bubbling energy erupted into an impulse, and I had a little butterfly "tattooed" onto my backside. I—who had waited until my daughters' ears were pierced before having the courage to have my own done, and who was still mildly horrified by tattoos on other people— was now acting on the new and incredible adrenaline rush of having wowed an audience.

The tattoo was impermanent, it washed off in a month or so as I knew it would. But for a little while I had been a few rungs higher on the ladder to happiness—which is usually a slow climb, two rungs up, one rung down, over a long time—and had a view from closer to the top, and I was thrilled to know that elation and great happiness existed, and that I could get there.

The following week, after my friends had left the camp for home, I went back to Old Orchard Beach to recapture some of the joy I had felt there.

It was different this time. I was alone among strangers who were milling around and talking to each other, but not to me. I took a walk on the beach, a wonderful thing to do alone. As I waded along the surf's edge, a motel that paralleled the beach was throbbing with music. All the sliding doors facing the ocean were open and the balconies were packed with college kids, drinking beer and singing. The radios in their rooms were set to the same station, so that the music blasted from about forty sets of speakers and washed out over the sand.

I remember the song, "Kiss Him Goodbye," and the sound of their voices joyfully belting out, "Na na na na, na na na na, hey hey-ey, goodbye!"

On the balconies, where kids in groups swayed and sang with their arms around each other, one guy stood out for me—red hair, sunburned face and chest, body like a linebacker, beer can in one hand, his other arm around his buddy's shoulder, singing with all his might—and I couldn't help it, I stopped walking and faced them, and swayed and sang, and celebrated with them for just a minute, before my loneliness punched in again and I resumed my walk.

If the night of the talent show had brought me four rungs up the ladder, now I was two down. It was O.K. Better than O.K. I was getting there! The joy of the kids celebrating together had reached me, infected me, and blessed me, and over time the memory of that scene has become one of my little treasures, and I still love that song.

Twenty-four

My first internship was at a mental health agency in Boston. Diane, my clinical supervisor, was a talented therapist, unconventional, spiritual, and she honored her own values without violating the strictly defined, insurance-imposed regulations. She didn't believe in diagnosing every client, thereby pathologizing their behaviors or reasons for seeking counseling. "It goes in their records, labeling them mentally ill whether they are or not, and most of them are not," she said, so she saw them for whatever they could afford, or for free. I was so happy to hear her express that perspective, especially having been a client myself for seven years. I was still seeing Grady for encouragement, support, and help with juggling the demands of my busy life, my ongoing grief about Becca's death, and my confusing relationship with Nick.

Diane also did not allow me to take notes during client sessions. "Give them your *full* attention," she instructed me.

"But I need to remember what they say," I objected.

"You'll have no trouble remembering what's important," she said, and those words burned into my mind and became a self-fulfilling prophecy.

My first client was a sixteen-year-old girl whose mother had called saying that her daughter had behavior problems and needed therapy. Diane set up an after-school appointment for me to meet with the mother and daughter together.

I was nervous. "I've never done this before," I told Diane. "I don't know what to do."

Diane smiled. "All you're going to do for starters is meet them, and begin a relationship. You know how to do *that*, Sam."

Oh, if that's all I have to do, I thought. *I know how to meet people, start a relationship.* I felt a little more competent.

I greeted my first clients (not *patients,* because they were not sick, and this was not a medical setting) in the waiting room and invited them into one of the small offices the staff shared. When the door closed, I felt "on stage" and my heart pounded. *Help me, God,* I prayed silently. *Please tell me what to say and what to do. Don't let them see how clueless I feel.*

According to Diane, all I had to do was make easy conversation and listen, something I had been doing all my life.

Their names were Laila and Jenny, mother and daughter, and they sat beside each other on vinyl-upholstered stackable chairs facing me. As I looked at them from the beat-up swivel chair beside the big, gray metal desk, I did a quick visual inventory: They were Asian, both pretty and well-groomed,—Mom with glossy black hair that hung to her shoulders, wearing a tailored suit, delicate jewelry and light lipstick, and teenage daughter with black hair cropped short and streaked with red, wearing designer jeans and heavy eye makeup. They both looked weary, frightened, and eager to ask anyone, neophyte or expert, for help. Given the setting, they probably assumed I was an expert.

I felt like an imposter.

"What brings you here?" I asked, directing the question to both.

Mom leaned forward to tell me, woman-to-woman, why she had brought her daughter for help.

"She doesn't obey me," she said with no trace of an accent, suggesting that she was American born, but I would ask about her background afterward. I knew that a parent's own life experience can greatly influence their expectations of their child. "She wastes time, she hangs out with kids I don't approve of, and she doesn't want to spend time with me anymore."

I remembered being sixteen, and I remembered my daughters at that age. So far it sounded like fairly typical behavior for a teenage girl. "What else?" I asked.

"The boys, they're the wrong kind, they're trouble, you know?"

I understood Laila's worry. Some of the boys Becca had hung out with were trouble, too.

"They drive," she continued, "and I don't want her driving in cars. I want her to come straight home from school, but she won't. She won't obey me!"

"It sounds difficult," I said. "Does Dad help with discipline?"

"He travels for work," Laila said. "He's in Hong Kong now. He's hardly ever home."

I looked at Jenny and saw anger flash across her face. I would need to find out more about that, too.

As Laila resumed the litany of her daughter's bad behaviors, Jenny tapped her foot, sighing, and looking down at the floor, apparently having heard all this many times before. In the child's body language, I saw anger and fear, rebelliousness and vulnerability. I switched my attention to her. "I like your jacket," I said, knowing from a lifetime of being daughter, woman, mother, how to engage a frightened girl.

She looked up and grinned. "My mother hates it," she said.

"Why?" I asked Mom.

"Because it's the way those other kids dress, the kids she shouldn't be hanging out with. I buy her nice clothes, and she swaps them with her friends and now she looks and acts like one of them. And she plays that awful music, I can't stand it!"

And so the conversation went. I found it easy to coax from them their individual perspectives about why they had come. "I'm sixteen," Jenny said. "I'm old enough to pick my own friends."

"She's still a child," Laila said, "and I want her to obey me."

Obedience. It had been at the center of my childhood and my teen years. My parents had been notorious among my friends for being extremely strict. Like Jenny, I was expected to be a certain way and become a replica of my mother, with one exception: I was to have a college education, and a "career to fall back on" if my husband couldn't provide luxuries. My mother pushed me to wear the fashions she liked and project a dignified image. I, of course, wanted only to be like all the other girls—sometimes sloppy and rowdy, other times mischievous and silly, and always wear whatever they wore, not what my mother chose for me. My parents gave me a solid upbringing, but at the age that Jenny was now, I didn't feel as though my life was my own.

I could also empathize with Laila. I had raised my own children with more freedom than I had grown up with, but we had still argued about choices and obedience.

As I looked at my first clients, I thought of Becca, and how a daughter's life can be taken so quickly, and I thought, *You're lucky to have each other.* Becca would have wanted to help them, and now I had the chance to do that for her, as well as for them.

Time flew by and we were startled when the timer beeped, marking the approaching end of the fifty-minute session. We set up standing appointments to continue meeting, sometimes for both of them together, sometimes just one.

When Laila came alone, I learned that her parents had immigrated from China before she was born, and she had been raised in the old ways of their country. She had tried to be a more modern American mother to Jenny, her primary companion in her otherwise lonely life, since her husband, who had been born in China, spent much of his time away on business. She had imagined that she and Jenny would be closer than she had been with her own mother, not be just mother and daughter, but more like friends for life. Jenny's growing up and becoming her own woman, with different values, was understandably threatening to Laila.

When Jenny had her private appointments, we talked about her friends, her clothes, and her music. One day I invited her to bring her favorite music to our next appointment, and I brought in my boom box from home.

When I heard the first song, as we huddled knee-to-knee by the boom box in the small office, it took me by surprise. It wasn't music at all, at least not to my ears. It had a loud, steady, thumping beat, and a male voice chanting over the rhythm in African-American dialect, more like spoken poetry, but in words I couldn't make out.

"It's rap!" I exclaimed.

"Yup," Jenny said.

"What are they saying?" I asked.

She shrugged. "I dunno."

"Then why do you like it?"

That grin again, and a coy flutter of her lashes as she dipped her chin but maintained eye contact. "Because my mother hates it."

I laughed. She laughed, too. Now we had a secret. She didn't like the music either, but it was a way to separate from her mother, and she was using it.

Although strict confidentiality protected my clients from being discussed with anyone else, the exception was that I was required to confer with Diane about my caseload. I referred to these clients as Mother and Daughter.

"I don't see any pathology in Daughter," I said. "She seems like a normal teenager to me. Am I missing something?"

Diane smiled. Although younger than I, she had worked with teens for decades. "Of course there's nothing wrong with her," she said.

"I think Mom is sad and worried, afraid of her daughter's growing up, possibly making bad choices, and especially because when

Daughter pulls away Mom is lonely, because Dad is hardly ever around."

"Yes," Diane said. "I think that's what's going on. Can you work with that?"

I was pretty sure I could. After all, I had lived it.

They came every week for the next several months, sometimes together, often separately. I liked them both and looked forward to their appointments. They talked, I listened, I told them I understood their frustrations and that their feelings were normal. I pointed out that Jenny was smart enough to know how to stay out of trouble, but still needed parenting, and that Laila, who was delightfully personable, needed to make new friends. We tried scheduling some appointments for Jenny's dad to meet together with all of us, but he never came, pleading demands of his business, giving me a feeling for how absent he was from Laila's and Jenny's life. They talked with me about missing him, something they had not done together before. They were learning to communicate from the heart—first with me, then with each other.

When my internship ended I referred them to continuing therapy with my successor at the agency. We were all sorry to say good-bye. They thanked me and said I had helped them, that they had learned things from me about communicating better, negotiating more, and recognizing their differing priorities.

From them I learned that being an effective therapist is being willing to listen without judgment and to share the appropriate parts of my experience, my training, and my thinking with people who are willing to change. I was learning that what I already knew, from having lived my life in the way I had and from being a client in therapy, could be of great use in treating my own clients.

That was the first time I experienced the not-knowing that occurs for a therapist following the end of our work together. I don't know, and may never know, how Laila and Jenny fared after we parted. Did Jenny grow up to eventually make her parents proud of her? Did Laila find new friends and create a full life of her own? Did they become close as mother and daughter, or as friends?

I hope so. I also hope I contributed some of what they needed for making all those things happen.

Twenty-five

The pace at school was breakneck, one course ending and another starting every five weeks, always with an exam or term paper due. The classes were stimulating and I loved my internship even more. Diane modeled the kind of clinical work I wanted to do, helping clients in any way she could, even helping them find jobs or giving them an occasional meal. She treated her student interns as generously and as supportively as she did her clients, following the principle of parallel process, meaning that how the supervisor treats the student is how the student will treat the client. It is a fundamental precept in clinical social work, particularly at BU, and was demonstrated with clarity in that agency. I was never judged or criticized, only advised. My strengths were nurtured. I was told what I was doing right and how I might want to change what wasn't working well. Being taught that way led me to treat my clients in the same way, and became the platform for building my clinical style.

In January 1992, the class was halfway through the grueling academic program and the faculty threw us a dinner party to mark our achievement and encourage us to hang in. After the dinner, some of my classmates presented a skit, giving everyone a hypothetical award: Most Studious, Drives the Most Miles To Class, Most Likely To Switch Careers and Become a Sky Diver, and other silly things at which we laughed uproariously because we so badly needed to kick back from the demanding pace for a couple of hours and have fun. When my name was called I walked to the podium for my prize, created especially for me, The I'm Not Really a Social Worker Award. Everyone, including me, cracked up.

———————

One of my part-time jobs was in a medical building connected to a hospital with a hospice program. I had wanted to do hospice work since 1983, when I was still married to Paul. That year, two of my closest friends were diagnosed with terminal cancer. The hospice movement that had begun in England had not yet made it to the United States, so Anne and Barry, single and wanting to avoid painful, treatment-driven end-of-life experiences, each needed to create a care team and arrange for palliative care on their own.

Anne's children came home from college to be with her, and I visited every week, helping her close out her life. I found a funeral director who would come to her home and help her arrange for her funeral, and I sat with her as her strength ebbed and she told me she knew she wouldn't live until her fiftieth birthday, only two months away. She was a therapist, and carefully prepared each of her clients for the end of their therapy with her. When she finally died, comfortably, in her own bed, I called each of her clients to deliver the news, as she had asked me to do.

Barry's death took longer, and a group of his friends formed a team to share in his terminal care. I brought him dinner every Thursday night and stayed with him until his son got home from work. Barry and I talked about life, his and mine, his sad and happy memories, our marital struggles. He instructed me in rolling the joints of marijuana that he smoked after I left, to ease his physical pain. With the help of family and friends, he was able to remain at home for a year and a half following his diagnosis, before he died in a chronic care hospital.

Accompanying Anne and Barry through their final days was a great privilege. I learned much from them about courage and acceptance, and the value of having someone to talk to at a lonely and frightening time of life. I had warm, loving memories of those precious last weeks, and I wanted to do it as part of my life's work.

I met the Director of the Hospice Program on the elevator going down to the cafeteria one day, and asked for an appointment to talk. Two days later, in his office, I made a proposal to him.

"I'll be needing an internship next year, and I'd like to do it in your hospice program."

"That's a great idea," was his response. "We've never had an intern, but I'd like to do that. Give me some time, I'll talk with the Director of Social Services, and see whether we can't come up with something for you."

I was steering my life in the direction of my goal.

Twenty-six

The days and weeks leading up to every anniversary of Becca's death were agony. I felt an increasing sense of tragedy about to happen. She was about to be killed, and there was nothing I could do to ward it off. The night before the date of her death was the worst. *Don't go there! Don't die!* I don't remember how I made it through the first two anniversaries, because my mind has blotted out the details of how I weathered that anguish. But as the third anniversary approached, I knew I had better make some plans to protect myself from the bludgeoning pain.

One of my classmates was a lay deacon in his Catholic church, and I asked him if he knew anything about Catholic retreats, which I had heard about but never experienced. With his enthusiastic and supportive instruction, I called a local abbey and requested accommodations for a private retreat for two days, so I could spend that terrible night in the peaceful safety of the convent. I said I would like spiritual direction, as my friend had recommended, although I didn't know what that meant.

For two days I walked the quiet grounds of the abbey, ate the simple meals the nuns prepared, enjoyed the calm solitude, listened to the nuns singing Gregorian chants in the chapel, and visited privately with Sister Miriam Pollard, who gently, wisely, comforted me and helped me learn to accept Becca's death.

After we had been talking for hours she asked, "If you could give it all up, never have been her mother, and never had to lose her, would you?"

To never have been her mother? "Absolutely not," I said, and realized that losing Becca was part of being her mother, that if her death was the price of the privilege of having been her mother, I would grasp it to my heart, with gratitude. She had been a blessing in my life. *I am her mother!* I told myself for the rest of the day, as I walked the paths through the woods by the abbey. *She is my daughter!*

I visited the abbey and met with Sister Miriam every year after that on the anniversary of Becca's death, and we became good friends. When she left New England to become the prioress of an abbey in the Southwest, we corresponded often, and many years later, when I visited Arizona, we would have a warm, affectionate reunion.

I had been introduced to the loving hospitality of religious communities that welcome travelers in search of spiritual comfort. For years to come I would seek and find a place of welcome among them, wherever I went.

In the list of elements I needed to make it into Category Three,—those who not only survive trauma and loss but also grow because of it,—I had gathered my support and identified my goal, but the second ingredient, something greater to believe in, was still eluding me.

I asked Grady, "Do you pray?"

"All the time," she said.

"To whom?"

"I believe in God," she said. "But that doesn't mean you have to."

"But if I don't believe in God, there's no one I can pray to," I mused.

"You can pray," she said, "if it feels good, helps you, even if you don't know who or what you are praying to."

So I started praying in earnest. I prayed steadily that the internship at the hospital would materialize, not sure who I was praying to but feeling that I was pulling in some energy from somewhere, to add to my own desperate hope. When the Field Placement Committee announced the internships, I was assigned the internship I wanted, the one of my own creation and the hospital's design: I would work on the medical-surgical floor mornings and with the hospice team afternoons, three days a week for the full academic year, until graduation in May.

I did not take this as proof that someone on high had heard my prayers and granted them, but more as an affirmation that praying had helped me hope and believe, and that hope and faith had helped me give it my best shot, and then await the outcome.

I lay down on a blanket on the floor and closed my eyes. Pamela covered me with another blanket and sat on the floor beside me with a pad of paper and a pencil. The music from her tape player began, a classical orchestral piece I didn't recognize, low and melodic, led by the strings. "Just tell me what thoughts come to mind. Let the music guide you," she said.

I listened and waited for thoughts to come. In a few seconds, they did.

"I am in a boat," I said, "sort of like a canoe, drifting down a river that flows from Maine to Florida, or maybe it's the coastline. I stop at a friendly town along the way. People welcome me, I stay. I make friends and become part of the community." I stopped speaking, listened to the flowing music, watched the scene in my mind.

"What's happening now?" Pamela asked.

The music took on a sad tone. "It's time for me to leave," I said. "Everyone is saying good-bye to me." I felt tears well up, and one roll down my temple into my ear. "I am climbing back into my boat, waving to them."

"How do you feel?" Pamela asked.

"Sad," I said. "I hate to leave, but I must."

"Why, do you think?"

"Because I'm searching for my place, my people, and they're not here. So I need to travel and look farther."

The music continued, softly, changing. In my mental image, I floated again in my canoe. "I've come to another village," I told Pam.

"That's good," she said. "Stay with it."

"These people are welcoming me, too. We're dancing together."

"Mmmm-hmm . . ."

"I love being with them. They are taking me into their community."

The music continued. I listened and watched the images in my mind that it evoked. "Oh!" I said.

"What is it?"

"Time to leave," I said. "I'm getting back into my boat. We're saying good-bye."

"Do you know why?" Pamela asked.

"It's not my place; this is not where I'm meant to be. I need to keep searching. I hate to leave them." Tears again.

I continued to describe my imaginary journey, with the music seeming to dictate the script of stopping, embracing new people, and saying good-bye, lots of good-byes. Finally, something shifted.

"I think I'm arriving," I said.

"Where?"

"At my Right Place. These are the people who have been waiting for me. They are receiving me with open arms. We're all very, very happy!"

"Now what?" Pamela asked after a few minutes.

"Now I stay. I'm home. I don't need to travel anymore."

The music ended on a joyful note and I opened my eyes, feeling drained, exhausted, and happy.

"What does it all mean?" I asked her when I had sat up.

"I don't have the answers," she said. "Except to tell you that there are many ways to experience that music, and your response is about you."

For days, even weeks afterward, I felt as though I had visited another realm, seen the future, received some inkling of the path I needed to follow.

———————

My new internship started in September. Mornings began with reading the medical charts of the hospital inpatients I had been assigned, to find out what may have happened during the night. Then I entered the room of each patient to inquire how they were doing. My role was to comfort and reassure them and their families about getting through whatever they were dealing with, and to make plans with them for the time immediately following discharge from the hospital. Some would be discharged to home, many would need to have a week or more of treatment in a rehabilitation facility, still others would need to go into a long-term care facility, and some would be going home with hospice care.

None of the patients I was assigned to had come into the hospital for a happy reason, such as the birth of a baby, but for a serious illness or injury, some requiring major surgery that they had not anticipated and didn't like at all. They were sad and angry, and the process of accepting their situation resembled the Kubler-Ross model of the phases of grieving. When someone has experienced any major loss, whether a home, a child, or one's health, especially if it happened suddenly as in the case of a stroke or heart attack, they are at first emotionally numb with shock, and then, when the reality of the situation sinks in, their emotions run the gamut of anger, sadness, trying to bargain with fate or God, depression, and ultimately acceptance—except that it doesn't happen as an ordered sequence, first, second, third, and so forth. It's actually more like a random ordering of all the possible reactions. Since anger feels energizing and helps to ward off the feelings of defeat that come with acceptance, it's the favorite response of some patients.

I was still on the same roller coaster ride myself, grieving for Becca. I was also experiencing another phenomenon of grieving that I call "falling into holes." Right after Becca's death I had felt as though I was in a deep, dark hole. Two years later, when I experienced my first hour of joy, riding along the shore with Carol, I thought I was out of the hole for good. But the next time I missed Becca, I fell into another hole. I walked the road of healing, falling again and again into deep holes that were placed farther and farther apart, but were always just as deep as the first one. What I learned was that although I would keep falling into them, I could always climb out, and walk a little farther before falling into the next one.

One patient, a heart attack victim, was angry and still in a deep hole. He asked me to leave his room and never come back.

I told Linda, my clinical supervisor at the hospital, that the patient had sent me away. She instructed me to go back to him and say that social services had a job to do, and there was no other social worker but me available to plan his discharge.

"Then please do your talking with my wife," he requested, and I did.

It was a great opportunity for me to work with a hostile patient and learn that his hostility was not really toward me. I needed to understand that his rage was actually at what had happened to him, and I was the ideal target. Just being with an angry person who doesn't have someone to blame is to volunteer to be that person's target. After Becca's death some of my friends had stepped into my "target" circle, and some of them couldn't take it, and others could take it for only so long. Being a social work intern, I had to learn to take it.

On Tuesday mornings, I attended the hospice team meetings and on the other days I spent mornings on the medical ward. After lunch I left the office and drove to the homes of my hospice patients to look in on how they were doing and talk with them about whatever was on their minds. Hospice service is for the families of the patients, too, so I often took a boy who was losing a parent out for an ice cream cone and a chance to talk, or took a walk around the block with another patient's sister. These families were all aware that death was approaching and little time remained. They wanted to talk, although

115

some people needed to skirt around what we called, in the offices of the hospice team, "the D word." I never used the words *death, die, or dying* before the patient or family member used them first, thereby indicating their readiness. But I could explore their readiness by asking questions like, "What's on your mind?" "What do you think lies ahead?" "Is there anything you're afraid of?" "What has your doctor told you to expect?"

The responses were varied, from "I don't know" and "Nothing" to "I'm dying," "He's dying," and "I'm afraid of dying." Sometimes a patient asked me, "Am I dying?" I was not allowed to answer the question directly because that was the duty and prerogative of the patient's doctor. I would answer, "What has your doctor told you?" I became very adept at feeling out the patient's emotions about their own imminent death.

Keeping patients' quality of life as high as possible, helping them plan excursions to the beach or into town for a show, was rewarding work. People who know death is approaching start their grieving early. It's called anticipatory grieving, and has all the elements of grief following a loss—denial, anger, depression, bargaining, acceptance, and falling into holes—but they are more open to receiving help with it, and the process is more gradual for them, although just as painful. I felt honored to walk with my patients and their families through that tender time.

One of the most sacred times was the moment of death. Most often, if the family had called hospice in ample time for us to prepare them, the patient died peacefully after each family member had said the things we helped them realize they wanted to say, such as "Please forgive me," or "I forgive you," and almost always, "I love you," "Thank you," and "Good-bye." After the patient took a final breath, the room would feel inhabited by an invisible presence of peace, and the family would be wide-eyed with surprise at how painlessly and peacefully it had happened. That internship in medicine and hospice opened a door for me into a special part of life that was intimate and holy. I was working for the sake of gentle kindness, for the forces of good, and for the memory of Becca, whose heart had always held strong love. This work called upon my ability to love, and I was grateful to be doing it. I had discovered a calling in me to work with people who are going through the most difficult times in their lives and need comfort, protection, and validation of their experience.

Twenty-seven

By that final year of graduate school, the brutal pace of working, serving two year-long internships, studying, and going to school seemed to have taken a toll on my physical strength. I became too tired to do it all. My doctor ran tests and told me the results were normal. "I think you're depressed," she said, "and your fatigue is psychological." She referred me to a psychiatrist.

"Sure, I'm feeling blue," I told the psychiatrist, "but it's because I'm discouraged, because I'm tired all the time. I don't think my fatigue is from depression, it's the other way around." Nonetheless, he prescribed antidepressant medication to try for a couple of weeks. When I went back to him, he asked me how I felt.

"More cheerful," I said, "but still exhausted." Increased doses and different medications did nothing more than create problematic side effects. He decided that my fatigue was a medical problem and discontinued the drugs. The crushing fatigue continued, and I pushed hard through it. I loved what I was learning and doing, and was determined to complete the academic program successfully. Solving the problem of my fatigue was just going to have to wait.

In March, my class was given the opportunity to visit Denmark as guests of the School of Social Work in Aarhus, where we would be students for a while, as part of an exchange program our school had with theirs. Twenty of us went, including four faculty members, to study the social service system and the role of the social worker in Denmark.

My hosts were a student named Annette, which she explained to me was pronounced "Ann-EDda", and her boyfriend, Espen. I slept under their dining room table on a thick, soft, fluffy, down-filled mattress (the traditional Danish guest bed), and despite my fifty-five-year-old, arthritic body, I slept very comfortably. Few people there had automobiles. Almost everyone, regardless of age, rode bicycles. I walked everywhere, and lost weight even while enjoying the rich Danish diet.

When I returned home, I realized I was more tired than ever. Somehow the excitement, novelty, and charm of Denmark had temporarily energized me, but now I was suffering utter exhaustion. I wondered whether I was going to make it until graduation. A few of my classmates had already decided the pace was too much for them and had made arrangements to "walk" at the graduation ceremony, which meant that they would cross the stage and accept what looked like a diploma, but would actually be a sheet of blank paper, and they would complete their course requirements in the summer and autumn sessions following graduation. That option was available to me, but I was feeling quite desperate to get on with my life—graduate on time, take the necessary exams, and do the required work under supervision to reach my goal of private practice in psychotherapy.

***

My part-time job that year, 1992, was teaching computer skills to children in private day schools in Boston and its suburbs. I woke up early to get to work on time, and stayed up late preparing lessons for the next class and doing my own homework for the weekend. Three days a week I reported to the hospital to put in a full day of my internship.

Another problem had arisen since the start of the academic year—I had become unable to swallow anything solid. Meat, fish, fruit, everything stuck in my throat and made me gag. More than that, it was painful. Consulting my doctor would have made sense, but I felt so pressured to work, study, and graduate on time, that I opted instead to live out the year on a diet of milkshakes, ice cream, yoghurt, and occasionally some pureed fruit or vegetables. I discovered that I could swallow better when standing, so I drank a lot of protein shakes and smoothies while standing at the kitchen counter. I brought shakes with me in a thermos when I left home, heading off to work, school, or my internship at the hospital.

By February my fatigue was overpowering me, and I had to quit something, so I reluctantly resigned from the teaching jobs. Although grateful for more time to sleep and study, I missed the income, so I took out a second mortgage on my cottage, with no idea how or when I would be able to pay it off.

I was focused on getting through the school year and desperate to graduate on time.

———— ·—· ————

"I have some news to share," Grady told me as we sipped tea in her office.

"Mm-hmm," I said, mildly curious. *A new office? A new schedule?*

"I'll be moving away in April."

Even though that was three months away, I was stunned and frightened. Grady had been with me through eight of the worst years of my life, and I didn't know whether I could function well without her steady support.

She saw the concern on my face. "We'll have lots of time to talk about it," she said, "and I'll refer you to someone with whom you can continue."

For the next three months, we talked about what her move away would mean to me and how I could continue to build on my new coping skills. Talking about it with her helped me understand that I could deal with it, and would do all right. Still, I was apprehensive.

———— ·—· ————

At school I barely made it to the finish line, physically, but my grades were all A's except for one A-, bringing my grade point average to 3.97. I knew it had been absurd for me to work so hard at the expense of my health, but I've never been very good at finding and maintaining the middle ground. I had felt driven to achieve this goal, and unwilling to risk failure.

Sasha was my date for my graduation dinner. Just before the meal, the director of the program suddenly realized she had forgotten to line up a speaker from our class. She went from table to table and eventually came to me and said, "Everyone says you should make the speech."

I went to the podium and told the story of being rejected for admission three years earlier, and how I had argued my way in. The audience seemed to find it hilarious. Then Dean Jones was introduced: "And now, ladies and gentlemen, the man who admitted Samantha White to the program . . . " and here there was more laughter, especially from me, because now I felt victorious. In two days I was going to complete the program, and on time!

Finally—commencement. My parents, daughter, brother, and sister-in-law came to share my joy. We had a celebratory lunch at a restaurant in Boston before going to the commencement site on campus. When my turn came to cross the stage, have the gold hood draped over my red robe, and receive my diploma from Dean Jones, a cry of "yay"s and clapping from my family prompted one of the professors draping my hood to say softly in my ear, "It sounds like you have a cheering section."

I did, and if I had had the energy, I would have cheered them, too. That graduation meant more to me than any other achievement in my life except becoming a mother, twenty-seven years earlier and then again, two years after that. I also had to include my marriage in the list of great and meaningful events in my life, despite its painful ending, because marriage to Paul had given me my daughters, both of whom were very much with me that day—Sasha in the seventh row, and Becca in my heart.

Now that I had the degree, I was eligible to take the state certification exam that was scheduled in two weeks. After that, I'd need to find a job. But all I wanted to do now was sleep.

Twenty-eight

I was still unable to swallow solid food. I believe I was stressed beyond tolerance, that my esophagus was in spasm because of it. More than anything, I had an urgent need to get away, far away, and to feel the distance from the demanding pace of the past three years, and from my parents. They had been wonderfully supportive of me throughout the process, even providing money for my tuition, but in their love for me and joy at my being with them, they had hovered, as they had done all my life, to the point where I felt strangled.

Everyone needs a way to escape stress, and my favorite—healthier and more fun than drinking, smoking, compulsive shopping, eating, gambling, or drugs—was travel. It may have classified as what is called "running," as in "running away," and I admit there was some of that, but I was going somewhere wonderful. I booked a trip by train across the country, from Boston to New Mexico, where I had never been, using the money from graduation gifts and a bequest from my aunt. I was nervous about spending three weeks on my own with no traveling companion, but pushing the boundaries of my comfort level had become my ever present challenge as a single woman. I wasn't going to let emotional discomfort rob me of a great trip. I figured I'd see a doctor about the swallowing problem as soon as I got back.

The train trip took forty-eight hours, and as I watched the miles, four thousand of them, roll by outside the window, I felt the tension in me slowly ebbing, my mind slowing down.

My first stop in New Mexico was at a remote convent in the desert outside Albuquerque, where I spent a week in silent retreat in what the nuns who lived there called a hermitage. It was a narrow room, with a private entrance from the outdoors, containing a bed, a writing table, and a refrigerator, with a small adjoining bathroom. My back door opened to an enclosed desert garden where I could be alone and meditate privately in the sun and silence. I had told the nuns about my inability to eat solid food, and they stocked my refrigerator with yoghurt, bananas, and applesauce, and prepared special meals for me of mashed potatoes, peas, and soft macaroni. Once each day I received spiritual direction from the abbess, who suggested I use my journal for dialogues with God.

"How would I do that?" I asked.

"Like writing a play with two characters. You write a question, and then you write God's answer."

"But how will I know what God would say?" I asked.

She smiled. "You'll know," she said.

I went back to my hermitage and opened my journal. *God, I* wrote, *Mother Celine said I should ask you questions, and you would answer. Is that true?*

I listened, and to my great surprise and pleasure, I "heard" God's reply, not in the form of an audible voice, but as a sudden and certain knowing that came through me, an inner wisdom that said, *Try it and see for yourself.*

I wrote that down.

O.K., I added, *what am I doing here?*

You came to unwind, relax, and heal from the stress of the past many years, especially graduate school, remember? My inner wisdom immediately responded.

I kept writing. *Yeah, that was a stupid question. O.K., how do I accomplish that?*

You are doing it now. You're in the desert, being cared for by the nuns, and you have no work to do, you can unwind and enjoy the sunshine, the desert, and whatever lies ahead in the coming weeks.

What will that be?

You'll find out as it unfolds. Don't worry about it, you'll deal with whatever comes up. Your agenda now is to unwind, period. Now would be a good time to take a walk to the chapel. Walk slowly, you are on retreat, no stress.

Thank you, I wrote, and sighed aloud. Of course, I knew all this, I had just lost sight of it. This was a technique I could use to "hear" what, in some deep part of myself, I already knew, but had forgotten. I had a new form of prayer.

That was when I began to understand one manifestation of "God" as a name for my inner wisdom. In time, I would learn that other qualities—love, compassion, generosity—could also be categorized under one word, one name, and although I could call it anything, the name God was short, easy, and all-inclusive of many strengths, blessings, and other good things, such as the loving hospitality the nuns at the convent extended to me that week.

For the rest of the week, I wrote and dialogued with my inner wisdom, asking questions and "listening" for the answers. I came to trust my gut, my intuition, as the wisest part of me.

In Santa Fe I stayed at a bed and breakfast owned by a friendly couple. Touring on my own, my eyes were filled with the rich color and beauty of natural historic sites, and I felt the strong presence of Indian culture. I visited the reservation at Tusuque on the day of the Corn Dance— impressive, solemn, religious, and moving—and stood for hours in silence broken only by the sound of the bare feet of the dancers shuffling on the sand.

The abbess at the convent had urged me to look up someone in Santa Fe, a natural healer who might help cure my inability to swallow. I met the healer in her adobe house near the plaza. After hearing about my problem she told me to stop wearing my favorite colors, magenta and purple, "compassionate colors" she called them, and switch to shades of blue and green, "the colors of self-care."

"But I have never worn blue and green," I told her.

"And you have never taken care of yourself, either. You will find that you look beautiful in those colors. Also, I want you to find a scarf or some beads to wear around your neck and over the upper part of your chest, where the tension has lodged, and its color should be teal."

"What does teal look like?" I asked, not sure I had ever seen it.

"Somewhere between blue and green," she said. "You'll know it when you see it."

After sending me to a nearby homeopathy shop with a note bearing the name of a remedy I was to place under my tongue three times a day, she wished me luck and told me I would soon be able to swallow easily.

I started taking the pills, and looked for blues and greens in the clothing and bead shops on the plaza.

From Santa Fe, I drove up to Taos, stopped at the beautiful Santuario de Chimayo just in time to hear Mass. Afterward I met the priest, who invited me to sit in the outdoor chapel in the pines behind the historic church.

I wanted to share the peaceful experience of sitting out there in the garden, and wished there were a way I could take a picture to bring home—of myself, sitting on the wooden bench, desert flowers at my feet, trees behind me. All I could think of was to place my straw hat on the bench and take a picture of that. The hat was sort of a "Symbolic Samantha," with its flowered, blue headband and wide brim that had become distinctively me. In the photo, the hat says that this is where I sat, but for me, it underscores my loneliness then.

In the village of Taos I sought out the pueblo and visited and had lunch with a young woman who lived there. Late that same day I went in search of Mabel Dodge Luhan's home, now an historic bed and breakfast, keeping her legend alive. She was an early twentieth-century writer and socialite who married a man from the pueblo, Tony Luhan, and described her coming to Taos and falling in love with him in her wonderful memoir, *Edge of Taos Desert*. I was so taken by the place—a three-story main house with attached guest accommodations, designed and hand-built by Mabel and Tony of blocks of adobe they made themselves—that I wanted to stay.

I was given a room for the night, Tony's room, in the main house, with its big, screened porch, and the bathroom down the hall where the writer D. H. Lawrence had painted the glass in the windows with blue and yellow geometrics. In the evening I watched videotapes in the living room made from the 16 mm. films Mabel and Tony had taken of each other and their friends, including the artist Georgia O'Keefe and D. H. Lawrence, clowning on horseback, laughing and posing for the camera, obviously enjoying being in the wonderful spot where I was now. I meditated through sunset on Tony's private porch, and then slept peacefully in his bed. In the morning, I enjoyed a huge and delicious breakfast in the dining room, sticking with things I could swallow, such as scrambled eggs and yoghurt, and then continued on in my travels.

For a short while, I had enjoyed a taste of the colorful life of some extraordinarily creative people, and that added to my adventure. Slowly, I was being drawn away from the pain of grieving and the stress of graduate school, and returning to a world filled with people and places that were thrumming with life.

I ended my retreat in the Southwest with a week-long spirituality conference at Ghost Ranch, in Abiquiú, New Mexico, a spectacularly beautiful area of towering red rock formations. I told the cook I needed liquids and soft foods, and she made sure that every meal contained something soft that I would be able to swallow—oatmeal, yoghurt, mashed potatoes, gravy, and applesauce.

At the ranch and in the surrounding area, I saw the red rocks change color, deepening as the sun dipped, until they were flames against a dark blue sky filled with stars. Their effect was literally staggering, and left me dizzy. I saw cottonwood trees and tumbleweeds for the first time, and felt a sense of space all around me that allowed my tight, protective shell to fall away, so I could expand into the space. I also made new friends among the other people who had come alone.

On the third day there, I joined some others for a ride on the Toltec Railroad, through the mountains to Chama, where we had a half hour before the train would start back down the mountain.

Opposite the train station was a little storefront with a sign reading, "Chama Mall." Some men were napping on benches under the sign. We were amused, it was so tiny, so sleepy, and nothing like the shopping malls we were accustomed to.

Inside, the mall consisted of four shops. Two of them were closed. One of the open shops displayed the wares of a local ceramicist, and I went inside.

My sight landed immediately on a necklace on a display stand facing the door. It was made of glazed squares of clay decorated with small brown feathers. It was beautiful, and the clay squares spoke their vivid color to me. Just to be sure, I asked the woman, "What color is this?"

"That's teal," she said.

I had to buy it, along with the matching earrings, and wore them back to the ranch.

At the conference I met a woman from Colorado named Nina, and as we talked, we discovered that we had a lot in common. She said she felt as though we were related, like distant cousins. She had arrived at the ranch in her car, and we both wanted to visit the Monastery of Christ in the Desert, so we drove out together the next afternoon. We found the entrance to the monastery and drove slowly for miles over the rutted dirt road to a dirt parking area among a few low, adobe buildings. A peaceful quiet pervaded the place, monks passed us and smiled but did not speak, and for the hour or so we were there neither Nina nor I felt the need to say anything. We rested in the shade of a piñon pine, soaking up the peace and beauty of the desert, and in the tiny gift shop bought audio tapes of the chanting of the monks. When we stepped into the chapel, we found ourselves facing not the usual stained-glass window of churches back home, but a high wall of clear glass that looked out at the towering red stone cliffs topped by puffy, white clouds in the blue, blue sky. My breath left me, I couldn't blink. I felt the spirituality of this place, this trip, this Earth. Nina and I lit candles and sat in silence to feel the sacredness, some sort of presence, of love and caring and connectedness.

This must be what God is, I thought. *This connectedness, this goodness.*

In one of my favorite photos of myself, which Nina took as we were leaving, I am leaning against an old piñon pine on that dusty road, wearing my new teal necklace and earrings, and my eyes are soft with deep, inner peace.

That evening I thanked the cook and told her it was no longer necessary to cater to my special needs. I could finally swallow again, and eat everything.

Twenty-nine

At the end of the summer, back from New Mexico, I landed two part-time hospice positions and found a new therapist, Beverly, also a clinical social worker. She was running a therapy group, so I joined and learned a lot more about myself in relation to others. My fatigue, however, was becoming relentless. I could not stay awake, even when driving from the hospice office to the home of a patient, or home from work. Many times I had to pull the car over to the side of the road to nap for ten minutes before I could continue the drive of only thirty-five minutes.

By spring Marilyn said, "Sam, there is definitely something wrong; this kind of fatigue can't be explained by just how hard you've been working."

My primary doctor referred me to a gynecologist who wanted to run some tests.

On a Friday afternoon in May, as I was getting ready to leave work, I received a phone call from her.

"Are you somewhere where you can talk?" she asked.

I said yes.

"Are you sitting down?"

"Yes," I said, puzzled by this way of starting a telephone conversation.

"Do you have a pencil or a pen and some paper?" she asked.

Oh, God! I thought, suddenly remembering. *Please, no, don't let her tell me I tested positive for HIV!* Working in hospice, where some of my patients were dying of AIDS, I routinely asked to have the HIV test included.

But she wasn't talking about blood tests. Something about the endometrial biopsy she had done, which I had completely forgotten about as soon as I had left her examining room to keep a lunch date with a friend.

So I wasn't HIV positive. *Thank you, God!* But apparently something else was wrong. "Tumor," she said, and "Uterus. Malignant. Urgent. Surgery." A sound like rushing water began somewhere in my head, making it harder to hear and impossible to think. I wrote as she spoke. She had contacted the best gynecological oncologist in Boston and he was expecting to hear from me. His name. His phone number. "Important to get into surgery quickly," and I was to call him as soon as possible. More words. "It can be cured," and "need to move fast," and "if we are lucky enough to have caught it in time."

I was alone in the dark office, where my desk sat outside the cubicles, pushed up against a flat, beige wall near a small, high window. The other hospice social worker, the volunteer coordinator, and the chaplain had all left for the weekend.

I walked slowly into the reception area where two secretaries were getting ready to leave. They stopped talking when they saw me standing there, clutching a trembling piece of paper, staring at it, looking, I suppose, perplexed.

"Are you O.K., Sam?" Elaine asked.

I squinted at the paper. The words swam on the page, made no sense. "My doctor just called," I said. "I have . . . " I read it aloud, "cancer." *Yes,* I thought, *there's that word, I must have cancer, because that's what I wrote, so she must have said that.* Still, I wasn't able to believe it.

They both rushed to hug me. "I always thought Friday the 13th was my lucky day," I wailed.

"But it *is* your lucky day," Elaine said. "Because now that you know you have cancer, you can get rid of it and be cured. If you hadn't learned of it, that would be *unlucky.*"

Good point, I thought. *Let's hope we can get rid of it.*

———————

When I left work I headed over to a reception marking the opening of a new clinic.

The room was crowded with people wearing nametags and milling about between a beverage bar, lots of chairs, and a big table laden with platters of cheeses and crackers, salads and breads, chips and dips. The mood was high and cheerful, the end-of-the-work-week chatter punctuated by greetings and easy laughter. Someone handed me a nametag. I pasted it onto my lapel, along with a smile on my face, and helped myself to a cracker stacked with cream cheese, cucumber, and a squiggle of anchovy paste, and took a glass of white wine. I headed for the row of folding chairs against the wall and sat down beside a young woman who smiled at me. She leaned forward to read my nametag, introduced herself, and told me she was a music therapist. "Tell me about yourself," she suggested.

"I just found out an hour ago that I have cancer," I responded brightly.

Her eyes widened and she was silent for a few seconds before asking, "Are you in shock?"

"I don't know," I said. "I guess so."

After about twenty minutes of holding the smile, I left and drove to a concert I'd been looking forward to, a famous traveling gospel choir performing at a church, but when I arrived the parking lot was empty. *What's this?* I wondered. *Am I the only person who likes gospel music?* I walked to the entrance and pulled a door handle. It didn't budge. I tried another door. Locked. *Is this Friday?* I wondered. *Am I early? Late? Have I missed the concert? Or am I now losing my mind?*

Then I saw a poster on the door, with a picture of the gospel singing group and the date and time of the concert. "Friday night," it said. "May 20." It took me a few seconds to calculate that I had come a week early, that the concert was next Friday. I stood on the lawn outside the brick building in the darkening spring evening, trying to figure out what to do next. I could go home, but I didn't want to be in my cottage, only a mile from where I stood, and be alone. Although the cottage and the pond had brought me peace, right now I knew they couldn't. What should I do? What is one supposed to do when they've been told they have cancer?

Finally it hit me. I needed some help with this. Maybe I should share my news with someone in my family, someone close to me.

A short while later I sat beside Sasha on the couch in her living room, and told her. I saw fear in her eyes. "I'm sorry," I said, and we wept together.

Thirty

I eventually went home, but couldn't sleep that night. I lay in the middle of my beautiful iron and brass bed in the darkness, watching the pale café curtains lift and fall on the breeze from the pond, like wings.

My cousin Stephen had died of cancer when we were only in our thirties. I remembered giving him his last haircut when he didn't have the strength to lift his head off the pillow. It was August and hot, and he said the hair on the back of his neck was uncomfortable. I had to vacuum the bedsheets around him afterward. We had laughed at my clumsiness, at the awkwardness of the whole scene, not saying aloud what I suspect we were both thinking—that the undertaker would see his haircut soon and be appalled by the raggedy job I'd done.

Because palliative care wasn't available then, Stephen had suffered. At his funeral I was overcome with loss, remembering how much we had shared since childhood, how much I would miss him.

When cancer had killed my friend Anne, twelve years ago, she had been younger than I was now. I remembered our last weeks together as she grew thinner and paler, and the last time I saw her she had looked like a skeleton encased in pale skin, blue eyes sunken in her skull, and she could barely speak.

These were the things I thought of as I lay sleepless in the dark. By four a.m. I was exhausted, but I couldn't stay in bed anymore or tolerate the darkness. I turned on lights and phoned my cousin Judy, who is a nurse. "What should I do?" I asked her.

I waited by the phone until she called me back with lists of books, clinics, and resources for cancer patients, and I recognized every one of them as something I had recommended to my own patients. In my panic, I had completely forgotten that I was a medical social worker and already knew all this.

Even so, it didn't help. I paced. I couldn't focus on my usual weekend routine of shopping, cooking, eating, and laundry. Instead, I dropped in on Sasha again, then came home and called family and friends, with one exception. My parents. I thought all weekend about telling them. They lived only an hour's drive away, and I knew there was nothing they would not do for me. But when they were worried, even if it was about me, it was always me to whom they turned. This time, I would not be able to help and reassure them, and I knew I couldn't bear their fear added to my own. So I opted not to tell them until after the surgery, when I would know how advanced the cancer was, whether it had spread, if I would need more treatment, and the prognosis.

Given my usual inability to ask for help, I never thought to ask anyone to come over, to share a cup of tea or a walk. But on Monday morning I couldn't bring myself to leave the safety and comfort of my bed, my pillows, my flowered quilt and peach-colored sheets, and go to work. I held the phone against my chest and wondered who to call. I thought of Linda, my clinical supervisor back in my hospital internship, and dialed her office. I said, "Linda, I'm falling apart!" and heard her say, "Of course you are. You're the patient, now, Sam."

Yes. The patient. The cancer patient, not the medical social worker, and I am allowed to be afraid, even a little crazy. So I stayed in bed for most of the morning and thought. Now I could finally make sense of the overwhelming fatigue that had plagued me the past two years.

I really hadn't thought this would happen to me. I had done "all the right things"—psychotherapy, massage, other alternative therapies, the homicide support group—and I had cried and had the dreams. Still, the cancer came anyway. *How ironic*, I thought. *And in my reproductive organs again.*

I mentally cast about for something to hold onto, to help me get through what lay ahead. Then I remembered the book, *Coming Back*, which had been serving me so well since Becca's death, and the formula I had adopted for transcendent healing that would move me forward: the combination of support, belief, and a goal. My therapists, friends and family had, so far, been my support. I had continued reading *Daily Word* every morning as a form of prayer, and begun to develop a concept of God that I could embrace. But now that I had completed graduate school, I needed a new goal.

I remembered a music store where I often stopped when I had an appointment with Beverly. It was a dark, narrow space, packed with sheet music and tapes, drums and electronic keyboards, with used

131

guitars, banjos, mandolins, and horns hanging from hooks on the unpainted pegboard walls, and a glass case filled with tuners, picks, sets of strings, and things I couldn't even identify. Piano lessons in childhood had taught me how to read music, but lessons stopped when I was fifteen and became busier with school, work, and dating.

The last time I'd been to the music store the man at the register had asked if he could help me. I felt obliged to say something and came up with, "Do you ever get a folk harp in here?" It was an instrument that had always seemed especially beautiful and sweet-sounding, the music of angels.

"Not usually, but a guy just dropped off a kit for one," he said. "You'd have to build it yourself."

"How much?" I asked.

And though I hadn't bought it, it had stayed on my mind. I had never built anything in my life, and I didn't know a thing about harps. But my friend Judith lived close to the store and now I called her.

She arrived at my house carrying a big, battered, brown cardboard box with multiple crossed-out mailing labels, indicating it had moved around a lot. We opened it together.

"Oh, Sam," she said, despair in her voice, "this is going to be impossible. Look at this—it's not a kit, it's just a big mess of stuff."

The box held a jumble of chunks of wood and metal, roughly cut and of different colors and types. Dozens of metal pins of various sizes rolled around on the bottom, beneath a tangle of nylon strings. Nothing looked anything like a harp. Who knew if all the parts were even there? I gingerly sifted through the mess, looking for instructions. There, a piece of paper! The print was small and faded, but showed a hand-drawn sketch of a finished harp shaped somewhat like a valentine. Dimensions noted beside the sketch indicated the finished instrument would be two feet tall, about right for being held and played on one's lap. It was a classic harp, and potentially very pretty.

O.K., I thought, *this is going to be a much bigger job than I imagined*. But I decided that after the surgery, during my convalescence at home, I'd build it, and then I would teach myself to play.

I was planning to live.

Thirty-one

My operation went well. The surgeon told me we seemed to have caught the cancer before it had metastasized, but that he would follow me closely for five years. For now, all I needed to do was go home, rest, and recover.

I told my parents that the problem had been cancer but the danger was past, and gave in to their urgings to convalesce at their house for a week. In their eighties, they were too frail to manage my medications and do for me the things I couldn't do for myself. Getting back home a week later was a relief. As Sasha drove me into the driveway beside my cottage, where the tulips were beginning to bloom, I was greeted by signs taped to the split rail fence—nineteen pieces of colored poster paper, each bearing one letter in black marker, spelling out WELCOME HOME SAMANTHA. It was a heart-warming sight and I wondered who had placed them there.

Nick and I had remained in touch—he had continued to call me almost daily, and had visited me in the hospital—and that night he came over and offered to stay. He had made the welcome home sign. He slept on the couch, to be available to bring me pain medication, breakfast, and the knowledge that help, if I needed it, was just a few steps away.

Over the summer I rested and followed doctor's orders to stay home for eight weeks before returning to work. During that time I studied the pieces of the harp and tackled the project in little bits, and by the end of my convalescence I had something that was beginning to look like a harp. I was eager to hear its first sounds, which wouldn't be possible until it was completed—assembled, varnished, pinned, strung, and tuned. I still couldn't see how this mix of wood and string was going to produce actual music, any more than I could have made a stuffed animal toy into a real, live puppy.

The woman in Louisiana died. Nick came to my house and I comforted him as he wept. I waited for him to propose marriage again, and monogamy, to me. He didn't.

———————

The hospice where I had been working the most hours replaced me while I was recuperating because, they said, they needed someone to perform my duties and could not wait for my return. I was still very tired and needed an income. My cottage was in urgent need of repairs—the roof was leaking and the sills were rotting. Owning it was costly and tied me to the local, saturated job market. I still loved my home and its view of the pond, but I was wondering whether it was the best place for me to be. I had prepared myself for Right Livelihood, but now I was thinking I also needed Right Place. Deciding whether to sell and move away, or keep my cherished home, was difficult. I had wanted to be in the house for life, and to bequeath it to Sasha, who loved it, too.

I had an inspiration: "Here's your inheritance," I told Sasha, "so you won't have to wait until I die." We arranged for the transfer of the house to her for the amount I needed to pay off my debts, and I moved out, comforted by her assurance that I could come back to visit whenever I wanted. Then I packed a few of my belongings into my car, stored my furniture in my parents' attic, and was ready to "hit the road," following the changing latitude of the sun as summer ended and autumn began, driving south, seeking my Right Work in my Right Place.

My harp had taken shape, and looked beautiful. I had installed the strings across the frame and I was looking forward to bringing it with me. The night before I was to leave for the starting point of my odyssey—a small convent in Maine, where the nuns were expecting me as a retreatant—my friend Louise called to tell me she needed to take one more measurement of the harp for the case she was making. I jumped into my car with it and drove the five or six miles to her house, and came home that night with the harp in its beautiful case of forest green canvas lined with plush rainbow-striped fleece. Before going to bed I checked the harp once more, strumming my fingers across the strings, which—although assembled of only chunks of wood, bits of metal, and lifeless strands of nylon—miraculously made lovely music.

Then I gasped and held my breath in horror. The last little piece of sanded and varnished wood that needed to be glued to the top of the harp, to complete its form, was missing. I searched the case. Nothing there. I searched the sofa, the table, the floor, the whole room. Nothing. I called Louise and she looked over the area where we had been at her house and reported back to me: no sign of the top piece of the harp. While she had been combing her house, I was out at my car, looking between and under the seats and on the pavement of the driveway. That harp symbolized my very survival, and I wanted it as my traveling companion while I would be living out of my car for as long as it took to find work and a new home. But I couldn't think of any more places to look for the missing piece.

That night I went to bed consumed with the need to find it. By now, from reading *Daily Word* and practicing prayer, I had begun to form a personal sense of what I was still calling, for lack of a better name, God. And so I prayed fervently for help in knowing where to find the little piece of wood that felt so important to me.

I fell asleep and dreamed:

I am standing at my bedroom window in daylight, looking out across a field. In that field, far from the house, is an object that I want very much, but can't see, because it is too far away and obscured by tall grass. I walk down the stairs, out the door, and straight across the field to the spot where I know I will find it, and I do. I pick it up and carry it back home.

I awoke from the dream just as the sun rose, threw on some clothes, laced up my sneakers, and set out on foot along the route to Louise's house. There were no other people and no cars, I was the only person out this early, so I walked in the road, looking to either side of me. I hoped I had absent-mindedly placed the piece of wood on the roof of my car last night before driving off, and had forgotten it, as I had done a few times before with books, and once with a saucepan, as people do when they're trying to focus on too many tasks. I watched the ground and walked.

About a half mile from home I saw something in the middle of the road, too far off to identify, but my heart sang, *That's it!* I didn't hurry my pace, just walked, as I had in my dream, and the closer I got to it the more it looked like the missing piece of my harp. I reached it, picked it up, held it, stared at it, folded my fingers tightly around it and said, *Thank you, God!*

I turned around and walked home, and glued the final piece onto the top of my harp, which at that moment I named Mira, short for Miracle.

135

After the good-byes, I started out on what Sasha teasingly referred to as "the geographical method for breaking off with Nick." He had not accepted my insistent declarations that we were no longer a couple, and I was too ambivalent to enforce them. I didn't trust or believe him anymore. He didn't share my values of openness, truthfulness, and commitment, and I knew I could not spend my life with him. But since he had returned from New Orleans following Becca's death, he had always remained available to me, helpful and supportive, which took on more value as other friends drifted away. Maybe distance between Nick and me would finally free me from his hold on me, but that was not my motive. I was moving because I needed work and a home I could afford.

Thirty-two

My first stop was at a convent on Peaks Island in Casco Bay. I looked for job vacancies at the Maine Medical Center and went for an interview at Portland Hospital, taking the ferry from the island to the city and thinking how much I would love to live on an island and commute to work by ferry every day.

There at the convent I had my first panic attack. I woke in the middle of the night and sat bolt upright, feeling lost and afraid, and as though I was dying, but worse—because death would have brought relief from the feeling. But there was no death, and no relief. For the first time, I felt my homelessness, and realized that being homeless was not just about not having a place to sleep and food to eat, because I had that, but about not having anyplace to go back to. I opened the window and breathed the salt air until the sun rose. In daylight, I was no longer afraid.

Apart from the time devoted to my job search, I spent hours every day by the ocean, drinking in the sunshine. I sat with Mira on the rocks and listened to the song the wind made as it blew through her strings. I practiced playing simple tunes—*Twinkle, Twinkle, Little Star*—and improvised tunes of my own. Peace and healing that I had long been needing crept into the empty places in my heart. I thought about Becca.

One evening at supper in the convent, one of the other retreatants said, "I was on the beach today, and I heard harp music. It sounded like angels! I looked up into the sky, and then out across the water, and finally I looked up and down the beach, and I saw you, Sam, sitting on the rocks, playing your harp. You looked and sounded like an angel come to Earth."

The next day, when I was sitting on the rocks again, I glanced down at the sand and saw a big, heart-shaped rock. It was the same size as the heart-shaped rock Becca had found at Acadia National Park when she was a little girl. I had taken my girls and a group of their friends on a hike through the forest. All the girls were finding rocks they wanted to carry home, and as they grew tired they each asked me to carry their rocks for them. Since I was tired, too, and wanted to be fair to them all, I told them they could take only what they could carry themselves.

Poor little Becca, the smallest of the children, had fallen in love with the heaviest rock. Stopping, starting, panting, and grimacing, she lugged it all the way home, where she painted it red and kept it in her room, always visible.

When she died, I found her red heart rock among her treasures, and felt guilty for not having carried it for her. When a child dies, most parents feel guilty for things done or not done, and I was no exception.

This rock, now at my feet, seemed a gift from Becca, and a means of atonement. I picked up the rock—it was very heavy—and carried it back to the convent, not by the route I had come, but by the long route, walking away from the convent and around the entire island, back to the convent by circumnavigation. It took me over an hour. With every step I said silently, *I'm sorry, Becca. I'm sorry I didn't help you carry your rock.*

The rock now decorates my garden, and has been joined by what has become a collection of heart-shaped rocks, some of which I found myself, others gifts from clients and friends who know I collect them.

Still feeling exhausted and mildly ill following the cancer surgery, I planned to drive for no more than four hours a day, and no two days in a row. From Maine, I drove to Newport, Rhode Island, where I stayed for more than a week with nuns in a convent on the Cliff Walk, in a quiet room with only a bed, a chair, a desk, and a stirring view of the ocean and the surf crashing on the sea wall right outside my window. I searched the newspapers for job ads and the telephone book for hospitals and hospices, typed letters on my laptop and printed them on my portable printer, and went to job interviews.

I couldn't play the harp at the convent because silence was maintained there to support the retreat environment, so I walked along the sea wall with Mira to the Music Department at nearby Salve Regina College and was given permission to use their practice rooms.

I was invited to a job interview a three hour drive away, in Connecticut, and I figured I'd present best if I showed up after a good night's sleep, rather than a long drive. I arranged to spend the night before the interview with some nuns nearby. Their guest house was a lavish summer home almost a hundred years old, on Long Island Sound, bequeathed to the nuns by a wealthy heiress. My room was on the top floor in the old servants' quarters, tiny but sweet, and furnished with antiques and lovely, soft matching sheets and towels. After watching television in the library, I climbed the long flights of stairs to my room and fell asleep pretty quickly. I slept well until I woke at around three a.m., needing to use the bathroom.

When I returned to bed a few minutes later, I lay awake and began to notice how my unfamiliar surroundings felt in the middle of the night. There I was, four long stories up, in a tiny garret of a room with two small windows that didn't open, and were so high on the wall that I couldn't see out. The ceiling sloped so steeply that it crossed the room from one wall to the floor. The parking lot, and my car, seemed far, far away down below me. At first I felt like Rapunzel, locked high up in a tower with all her hair cut off. Then I felt like the kidnapped heiress who, in the 1970's, had reported being buried alive in a casket, with only a straw through the lid to allow in enough air for her to breathe.

That's when I had my second panic attack. I was becoming crazed with claustrophobia and couldn't bear to stay in my room. I pulled on my robe and sandals, grabbed my journal, pen, and flashlight, and escaped downstairs to the porch, only to find that it was sealed off with heavy plastic. So I went outdoors onto the terrace overlooking the water, and breathed and relaxed, until the sun began to rise, and I was able to return to bed and to sleep. A few hours later Sister Christina rang the buzzer in my room to wake me for an elegant breakfast, served on a lace tablecloth under crystal chandeliers, by nuns in full habit. I was hardly the product of the restful night's sleep I had hoped for.

Even so, the job interview went well and they appeared interested in me. But I didn't want to live and work in the urban area they served, with its high crime rate, so we agreed to get back to each other and I returned to Newport, where Sister Evelyn, in khaki chinos and a polo shirt, put a casserole on the kitchen table for me. No lace tablecloth, no crystal chandeliers, just the formica tabletop and the ocean breezes coming in through the screen door. After I had cleaned up my dishes and taken a walk by the ocean, I felt as though I had come home.

Throughout my trip I explored work opportunities and stayed where hospitality was available to the traveler needing quiet space in which to pray, heal, and think. At each convent, monastery, or ashram I told my hosts of my history and my quest, and asked for and received spiritual direction. I always received loving responses, simple meals, and even referrals to places to stay farther along my route. And I learned that I am not a city girl, but a woman who needs peace, fresh air, quiet space, and preferably a large body of water very close by.

———————

I followed the coastline as I made my way south, looking at the ocean as often, and for as long as I could, drawing comfort and hope from it. The following week I stayed in New Haven with two of my cousins whom I hadn't seen since childhood, and felt fed by our shared memories and strengthening connection. In Cape May, New Jersey, I kept a date with a man I knew through our shared experience of having lost a child, and we had dinner together, then went our separate ways.

I took the ferry across Delaware Bay. The day was clear and beautiful, as all the days had been since I struck out on this voyage down the coast, the sky deep blue, the sun warm and soothing, the ocean breezes invigorating. From the ferry landing I drove down the Delmarva Peninsula, incorporating parts of Delaware, Maryland, and Virgina. The season was autumn, my favorite, with its sunny days, cool nights, and changing colors. The sandy soil, scrubby foliage, and smell of salt air reminded me of Cape Cod, where I had spent much of my childhood and still loved to visit.

I stopped at Chincoteague, Virginia, in the Assateague Island National Seashore, and checked into the only motel in town—small, inexpensive, clean, and hospitable. Only the locals were there this time of year, the tourists had all gone. I walked to a diner for my supper and then, back at the motel, snuggled in with a good book. I planned to spend the following day at the National Wildlife Refuge.

After breakfast I set out to explore the island in my car, and was surprised to find myself uncomfortably aware of being alone. I had been with the nuns in Maine and Rhode Island, my cousins in New Haven, and my friend in Cape May, but now I was traveling solo. I stopped at the entrance to the wildlife refuge and looked in at the long footpath into the dark woods, and felt frightened. I didn't know whether this was considered a safe place for a woman alone, but I knew I wasn't ready for it. I decided to continue my exploration from the safety of my car and drove on. I was feeling more alone and rootless, and farther from home and family, than ever before. I didn't know yet whether this trip was a good thing or a bad one. I was committed to doing it, but I was not totally at ease.

The following day I reached the end of the peninsula, loving every mile of scenery, and crossed the spectacular Chesapeake Bay Bridge for the first time. I am in awe of beautiful bridges, and this one was so incredible, arching over the water and then diving down into it to become a tunnel, and then back up again to where the road rose high above the water, still taking me southward.

Virginia Beach in October was deserted, the air cool, the sky clear and blue. I was the first to arrive at the beach house for a weeklong training in Guided Imagery in Music. I was going to learn the techniques of musically guided imagining that Pamela had practiced on me three years earlier. When I had planned this journey from Maine to Florida, I thought it might be a fulfillment of the prophecy my imagery had contained, and that I might find my Right Place in Florida. But there was a surprise ahead, and the surprise was where my personal quest would actually end.

That evening eight of us, all women, began to get to know each other. For the next week we would live together at the beach house and receive about six hours of training every day in the musical imagery techniques. At the end of the week we would receive certification in using them clinically. Each day I had an opportunity to be guided and also to guide someone else. When everyone spent the afternoons on the beach, I went to bed, because I was still exhausted all the time.

I remember being guided, listening to the music and feeling like an eagle, or more like I was riding on the back of an eagle, flying very high. I could look down and see Earth far below me, and somehow I did not feel afraid, but gloriously triumphant. My troubles all looked small, and I felt very powerful. I also had the feeling of Becca being with me, showing me that I was strong and could fly, and that all of it—life, pain, even her death—was beautiful when viewed from high enough.

141

One morning someone in the house announced, "The dolphins are running!" and on that day I took a walk and saw my first dolphins in their natural habitat, gracefully breaching and diving only about two hundred yards offshore, appearing and disappearing again and again, arcs of silver flashing in sunlight, as the huge pods migrated southward ahead of me.

The week felt curative, and reassured me that I could feel strong and overcome my pain. When it was over, I continued on my journey south, still looking for my Right Place.

In Georgia, I stayed at a hostel in the swampland where a thick swarm of mosquitos attacked me as I climbed out of my car. About twenty people were passing through the hostel that night, and the atmosphere was open and friendly. I was the oldest person there. One man cooked a big dinner and we each chipped in a dollar and shared the meal. A woman younger than Sasha, traveling alone, poured her heart out to me. That night I slept in a treehouse.

I reached Florida the next day and stopped for two nights at a seaside cabin fixed up like a New England cottage, and then farther on at a motel with a balcony from which I saw my first shuttle launch just a stone's throw down the beach at Cape Canaveral. I was captivated by the spectacle of the lift-off, the heavy, slow rising of the craft into the air, the silver streak that followed it into the sky, arcing as it followed the curvature of the Earth. A minute or two later the ground under my feet rumbled and shook like an earthquake, rattling the glass in the windows. I found it so surprising and thrilling that I had to tell someone. I called my friend Carol back home.

"That's great," she said. "I've always wanted to see one of those."

Hearing the warmth in her voice and exchanging our tales of what was happening, for her at home and for me on my travels, helped me hold off the ever present demon of loneliness for the rest of the day, and beyond.

I traveled on to an ashram farther south in Florida where a candle-lit Hindu festival took place outdoors by the water every night. The night air was balmy. I sat with a hundred people on the grass, listening to the music and chanting for hours. I stayed in the home of Usha, a kind and generous young woman who was part of the ashram community. She shared with me her lifestyle centered around Indian

Ayurvedic medicine and fixed me tea in which floated a spoonful of clarified butter, or *ghee*, and it was delicious.

—————

All the way down the coast I kept my eye on my old friend, the Atlantic Ocean. I drove or walked or sat beside it in New Jersey, Virginia, Georgia, Florida, and points in between, and spoke to it— mostly silently but sometimes aloud. "Atlantic Ocean," I said, "we've known each other forever. I feel as though you are traveling with me, keeping me company, and you make me feel connected to my past and my future. You comfort me with your steadiness, the music of your sounds. I've never understood exactly why you mean so much to me. Maybe because you are where life arose; maybe you are the womb from which all of us were born."

Whenever I could, I climbed an empty lifeguard chair and gazed at the horizon, feeling the space and freedom to grow and change however my soul needed to. I felt less lonely there, by the sea, than I would have in a crowded restaurant, surrounded by tables of chattering couples, families, and friends, while I dined alone. The beaches felt more like home than anywhere I'd been since leaving my cottage on the pond.

The journey I was taking in my car was nothing compared to the journey in my soul. I was shifting inwardly, seeking a new shape for my life. The shattered self I was reassembling would be better than the one that had been broken, would be more authentically me.

Thirty-three

The farther south I traveled, the more job opportunities came my way. I was invited to join the staffs of two very busy hospice programs in Florida, and I hadn't even sent my resume to all the hospices and hospitals on my list.

But other, more compelling things were happening. For one, I was feeling more and more exhausted and ill. The swelling from my surgery in May had not subsided, and I felt lumpy, tender, and faint from the heat, although it was already November. I wasn't able to fit comfortably into my good business clothes, and was wearing a large, yellow sack of a dress to job interviews because it was the only thing I could wear, other than soft and stretchy knit pants and T-shirts. I had another panic attack in the middle of a starless night when it occurred to me that if I needed my family to come for me, I wouldn't know how to tell them where I was. I called my brother and left a message saying I was ill and didn't know whether to continue my search. I was afraid I needed medical help and family around me.

The flat land, the straight roads, the empty distances, and the hot, humid air of the South were new and alien to me. I missed New England, the hills and curving roads, the shade, and just the right amount of crowding. I was deeply homesick, not for my adult home, but for what I remembered from my childhood. What I wanted was the brisk and salty air, the sand dunes, the winding roads and change of scenery around every bend of far away Cape Cod.

Molly, a friend from Boston, had offered me her cabin on Cape Cod months ago. "I was going to close it up for the winter this weekend," she said when I called her, "but if you want to stay there, sure, I'll leave it open for you."

Before leaving Florida I spent a day driving around, exploring a strip of beach along the coast, and discovered a pink stucco bungalow far from the road, right down on the beach. I decided to stay there a few nights before returning to New England.

It was a funky place, circular, with an open interior containing a kitchen area, a '50s retro formica dining table with chrome chairs, some comfortable living room furniture, and large windows facing out to sea. A spacious bedroom with a large, comfortable bed, and an even larger bathroom tiled in marble, with a claw-footed tub and beautiful fixtures, took up the back of the bungalow. The combination of tackiness and elegance seemed charming for its incongruity.

The first thing I did after stashing my groceries in the fridge was drape my floral-print black shawl over the formica table, and add some beach grass in a small green vase and a candle I found in the kitchen cupboard, for instant ambiance. Then I fixed a mug of tea and a snack, and took them out to the lawn chair at the head of the wooden stairs leading down to the sand, where I had read that giant loggerhead sea turtles came to nest. I relaxed and watched the shore birds riding the air currents, diving for their supper, as the sky slowly darkened and the evening star appeared. It was quiet, beautiful, and perfect. I felt content to rest beside my lifelong friend, the Atlantic Ocean.

The following day the sky clouded over, rain began to fall, and the wind picked up, and by afternoon a raging storm was passing through. I sat by the television set and watched the meteorologists with their weather maps of the unfamiliar territory, and heard the newscasters announce that the bridges to the beach had been closed and several towns had serious storm damage. I didn't know how close those towns were to where I was, and whether I was in the storm's path. The situation felt strange, and the news broadcasts alarming. Outside, the wind was all wrong. In New England, storms generally come from the Northeast, are bitingly cold, and smell of snow. This wind was coming from the Southwest, was very warm, and carried the fragrance of the tropics. Birds faced into the wind, flying but making no headway, and I wondered whether they were as frightened and bewildered as I. The surf was wild, dark green, almost black, enormously high, and crashing against the seawall in front of the bungalow. Water began to seep in under the front door.

As the day darkened I saw a light go on in the bungalow next to mine. I was so relieved to know I was not alone! I wrapped myself in a jacket and ran next door through the rain, bucking the wind, and knocked on the door.

It was answered by an elderly man in pajamas, slippers, and a terry cloth robe. He was, of course, surprised to see me.

"Hello," I said. "I'm staying next door and I don't know what to make of this storm." My voice shook.

He invited me inside and introduced himself. He was a retired Navy captain visiting a friend nearby, he said, and he always stayed here when he was visiting. "Oh, this storm is nothing," he said. "I've seen much, much worse, and at sea, too. This will blow over, nothing to worry about."

I thanked him and ran back through the windy downpour to my bungalow, feeling somewhat reassured, and grateful for his presence and apparent lack of concern about the storm.

About a half hour later there was a knock on my door, and he stood there under a black umbrella, in neat slacks, brass-button blazer, and tie, as proper as a gentleman stopping by for high tea.

I invited him in, offered him tea and fruit, and we chatted for an hour or more about his career in the Navy, his travels, his family, his annual visits to this spot, and about my pilgrimage that was about to take me back to where I had started. His visit was lovely and calming, and when he said, "Well, I think it's time I toddled off," I thanked him warmly, walked him to the door, and watched him carefully make his way back through the darkness, protected by his umbrella.

I woke several times that night to check the water creeping under the door, adding more towels to sop it up and hoping I wouldn't be awash when morning finally came.

With morning came the sun, and the sea was dotted with dozens of surfers riding the towering waves left in the storm's wake. The birds were making headway again.

I took one more day to commune with the sea in the sunshine, and left the following day. I knew I was doing what was right for me. I needed to be near the ocean that had been at my side, and soothed my soul, for the past three months, but I wasn't healed yet. For that, I needed to go back home.

I didn't see my charming neighbor again after our conversation over tea, but I still remember him, sixteen years later, with gratitude and fondness. He had recognized a damsel in distress, and had nobly risen to the call of gallantry.

I drove from the Southeast coast to a town near Orlando and put my car on the AutoTrain heading to Washington, D.C.

In the dining car, I was seated opposite a middle-aged couple and we were joined by a man traveling alone.

"So," the woman across from me asked, "where are you two from?"

"I'm from Massachusetts," I said.

"I'm from Miami," the man beside me said.

"And how did you meet?" she asked.

"Just now," I told her, "when we sat down."

She looked puzzled.

"We're not traveling together," I explained.

"You mean you're traveling *alone?*" she asked me.

"Yes," I said. "And where are you from?"

"We're from New Jersey," she said with a wave of her hand. "But why are you traveling alone?"

"Because I like to travel," I said, "and I'm single."

"Oh," she said, shaking her head, "I would never do that. I couldn't."

"Well," I said, "having no one to travel with, my only options are to travel alone or not travel at all. And I'm not about to give up travel just because I'm alone."

The man beside me followed me out of the dining car after dinner, and we chatted and exchanged addresses. I felt flattered to receive a letter from him a few weeks later, but I never followed up on his invitation to get to know each other better. I had different priorities: I still needed a job, a place to live, and to feel better.

I arrived in Washington the following morning and spent a couple of days there with my friend Joseph. Then I drove north and arrived at my parents' house in Massachusetts just in time for Thanksgiving dinner.

Mira, my treasured harp, had been with me everywhere I went, and I had taught myself to make soothing, peaceful, hopeful music with twenty-two strings stretched across a wooden frame in the shape of a valentine. My valentine to myself and to whomever wanted to listen.

Thirty-four

I arrived at Molly's cabin feeling exhausted, set up my computer and printer, and continued to look for work, this time focusing on the Cape Cod area. As T. S. Eliot wrote, "And the end of all our exploring will be to arrive where we started and know the place for the first time." I was back at Cape Cod, the favorite place of my childhood. I revisited my old haunts, the beaches, the canal, the bridges. I saw the place through adult eyes, and loved it more for having left and returned. I feasted on the changing sky, the sea, the sand, the winding roads, the brush kept low by the sea winds that swept across the narrow land. I went to the beaches, and sometimes sat in the empty lifeguard chairs and gazed out over the water.

I went back to the beach where I had spent my childhood summers, which I hadn't seen for more than forty years. On a bright winter day, sunny and cold, the beach looked as I remembered it, but smaller. The horseshoe crabs on the sand could have been the same ones I had carefully stepped over long ago. I sat on the big boulder at the back of the beach and looked out over the rock jetty, and realized that it was the same jetty I had sat on as a child, that I had changed shape and size, but the rock jetty still looked the same. I walked the road from the beach to the cottages where my family had stayed, and was brought back in time by the sand along the roadside being blown across the pavement by the wind.

At night, in the cabin, which was so tiny that I used the trunk of my car as my closet, the movie in my head gave way to dreams, all of them variations on a single theme:

I am relaxing in the cabin, listening to the rain, missing Becca. Suddenly I realize that I haven't sent her my new address. No wonder I haven't heard from her! I picture her lost and lonely and am stricken with remorse and more guilt than I can bear. I jump into boots and a rain slicker and search an unfamiliar neighborhood where I think she may live. I find a phone and call Sasha, and tell her we must find Becca, so I can reunite with

*her and plead with her to forgive me for not having contacted her sooner. I
don't understand what Sasha tells me. Suddenly I'm back in the cabin,
agonizing over what a terrible mother I've been, how hurt Becca must be,
and how desperate I am to find her! A large brown bird swoops down from
the gray Cape Cod sky and perches on a tall piling outside the rain-streaked
window. An eagle! Birds remind me of Becca, and the eagle, in particular,
seems a symbol of her spirit, her soaring spirit, since she died. Oh! Is she
dead, then? Will I never find her?*

I struggled up from sleep. For a few minutes I lay suspended
between the dream and waking, hearing the rain outside the cabin,
feeling torn apart, needing to know which was the reality, until a
mixture of relief and unbearable sorrow washed over me. Relief,
because I knew I had not forgotten her after all, and she was not
waiting somewhere for me, feeling abandoned; and sorrow, because I
remembered why I hadn't heard from her, that she really was dead.
And that I will never see her again.

Almost seven years had passed since she died so violently that
night, and although the dreams were less gruesome and horrifying than
they had been, I was still victim to nightly intrusions of the pain of
grief. I would arise shaken and stumble through the morning. Hours
would pass before my equanimity returned.

———————

In addition to the dreams, I couldn't get comfortable in bed, and I
wasn't getting much sleep. I was very weak. I hadn't seen my
oncologist in three months, so I drove to Boston for a follow-up visit.

"I'm still so tired," I told him. "Something's wrong."

He said, "Well, I don't know what it is, but I can tell you it's not
the cancer, because the cancer is gone."

I found a new doctor on the Cape. He took tests and told me,
"There's nothing wrong with you. You need exercise. I want you to
walk for at least a half hour every day."

I drove the short distance to the Cape Cod Canal and parked my
car in the gravel lot at the end of the towpath, a seven-mile paved trail
for walkers, cyclists, and in-line skaters that ran alongside the canal. I
got out of the car and began to walk toward the path, took about ten
steps, but was too tired to continue. I never even reached the
pavement. I rested for a minute and made my slow and painful way
back to the car. How was I ever going to walk for a half hour?

I consulted another doctor. He said, "There's nothing wrong with you. I think it's psychological; you're depressed." He referred me to a psychiatrist.

A doctor in Boston had told me that, too. *Here we go again*, I thought. *He thinks it's all in my mind.*

The psychiatrist prescribed antidepressant medications, new ones, that did nothing for my lack of energy. "I don't think you have a psychiatric problem," he said after several visits. "I think you have something like Epstein-Barr virus, or chronic fatigue syndrome. If you'd like to keep taking the anti-depressants, if they help you stay out of a depression, that's fine with me, but I'm going to call your primary care doctor and tell him I think you have a physical medical problem."

I hoped that meant a solution was imminent.

But my primary doctor became enraged at the psychiatrist for suggesting he didn't know his medicine, and insisted that my symptoms, in the absence of test results confirming a medical problem, indicated, by default, a psychiatric issue. "There's no such thing," he added, "as Epstein-Barr or chronic fatigue syndrome as an illness."

Neither of them could help me.

In addition to the fatigue, I was now aware of pain that was mostly in my joints, but moved around, so that on one day I would limp because my left hip hurt, and the next day my left hip was fine but my right one hurt. I wondered whether I was so mentally confused that I couldn't remember which hip hurt.

I spent most of my time, when I wasn't looking for work, lying down. I found that the only place I could get comfortable was on the living room couch, where I could position my knees, hips, and shoulders above the spaces between the seat cushions and throw pillows, so that they were suspended with nothing pressing on them. I had wracking chills, but no fever. I felt helpless, and I cried a lot.

Thirty-five

Finally, six months after leaving my cottage on the pond, I found a job on the Cape, and shortly afterward was able to move out of Molly's cramped cabin and rent a condo with a balcony overlooking the Cape Cod Canal. My parents and my brother, Dennis, and his wife, Karen, helped me retrieve my furniture and winter clothes from my parents' attic. I had an address again, and no longer felt homeless. I could see the water from my new living room, and watch the tugboats, sailboats, oil tankers, and ocean liners pass by my windows and balcony, close enough for me to see into the cabins through the portholes. The beaches were never far away, and I could spend my lunch hours sitting on a lifeguard chair, overlooking the sea and scanning the horizon.

My new job was Coordinator of Jewish Community Services for Cape Cod, which seemed a bit of a joke at first, because I had stopped identifying with Judaism many years before. But the job listing had said, "Familiarity with Jewish customs and practices required." Having grown up in a deeply traditional Jewish family, I was more familiar than most people with the customs and practices. I needed a job, and if they needed me to participate as a Jewish person I could easily do so.

Two carloads of my friends from my old neighborhood in the woods by the pond drove down to the Cape one Sunday morning to welcome me back to Massachusetts. We went out for brunch and took a short walk in the sunshine on the towpath alongside the canal. Being back with my friends was wonderful.

On another Sunday, Dennis and Karen drove down, bringing kites, and we went to the nearest beach, where we flew them together. I felt great joy being with them, playing like a child, and thanked them.

"I really have been needing this happiness," I told them.

"Maybe you'll start having more of it now," Dennis said. "You've certainly paid your dues."

Paid my dues. Yes, I liked to think that I had finished paying the cost of being happy again.

———————

I enjoyed my new job, which quickly introduced me to the Jewish community across the Cape. The position made me highly visible, with my photo in the *Cape Cod Times* and a number of speaking engagements. Having been raised to be highly visible, and coached by my mother in the art of looking good, I threw myself into acting the role of a high-functioning, competent woman—which I was, in public. Once back in my condo, I collapsed in exhaustion and loneliness.

The two rabbis on the Cape served as consultants to my position, and so I came to know them. In Rabbi Elias Lieberman, religious leader of the Falmouth Jewish Congregation, which practiced Reform Judaism, I found a friend who shared some of my interests and values, and was active in the secular community as well as the religious. I was further drawn to his congregation by its learning programs. I took a class in Hebrew, a language I had tried many times to learn but had always found both frustrating and intriguing. What intrigued me was the same thing that frustrated me: the Hebrew alphabet. The letters are beautiful shapes, begging to be calligraphed and developed into art forms, each letter having more than one meaning—a sound, a number, sometimes a word. I was fascinated by their shapes, and worked hard at remembering their names and sounds. Learning words was even more difficult, but I enjoyed the mental challenge. I also joined a class that Elias was teaching for women wanting to celebrate bat mitzvah, the rite of passage not available to me as a girl of thirteen because women are not permitted that honor in the Orthodox tradition.

On Friday nights, to avoid being alone and bored at home, I started attending Sabbath services in Falmouth and was moved by the way Elias conducted them. I was finding, for the first time, the beauty of the religion into which I had been born.

———————

At my new rental condo, sleep was increasingly difficult and eating right was close to impossible, because pain and fatigue prevented me from shopping for groceries, standing in the kitchen to cook, and getting a good night's sleep. The only real meal I had each day was lunch, because my office was surrounded by restaurants. I bought a memory foam mattress, which helped a bit with sleeping, but soon it wasn't enough to cushion the pain in my body. I put an egg-crate mattress on top of that, which helped for a while. Meanwhile, the symptoms of sleep deprivation set in: impaired cognitive function, erratic digestion and elimination, and, of course, physical exhaustion. Getting out of bed, showered, dressed, and fed every morning wore me out. Luckily, my job was not physically demanding, and it gave me something interesting and stimulating to look forward to each day.

In addition to working for the Jewish Federation three days a week, I worked two days at a counseling agency on the mainland side of the canal. Both jobs were close to home, and because clinical supervision was available to me at both, the work was qualifying me for obtaining the highest level of licensure, which I needed to achieve my ultimate goal–my own private practice.

Nick came to visit me in my new digs. We hadn't seen each other in eight months. When he recited his line, "I feel like stretching out. Will you join me?" and went into my bedroom but I didn't follow, he must have finally understood that our relationship had changed forever. Although he seemed to want it to resume as it had been, for me our sexual involvement was finished. I had been too disillusioned, and was now too angry and distrusting of him, to feel inclined to be physically intimate again. Traveling and living out of my car all those months had finally given me the feeling of distance between us that took me out of the magnetic field of his raging sexuality. When he left that day, I felt freedom from the addictive behavior I had fallen into with him, and a tiny bit of sorrow for the loss of a significant romantic relationship that had raged like a wildfire for two years, and had taken an additional seven years to subdue and, finally, extinguish. We remained good friends for a long time afterward, but I could no longer let him own my heart.

Being on my own, I was learning that I was attractive enough, and that my lack of thick, glossy hair and perfectly symmetric features didn't matter as much as I had believed growing up. There were men who found me attractive, and I dated a fair amount, but I had an unerring knack for being attracted to men who were, for some reason, unavailable, inappropriate, or not interested in commitment. I had been hurt too deeply by Paul, and then by Nick, and was probably unconsciously avoiding giving my heart away again. I could lend it briefly, from time to time, but was not yet willing to give it over completely. I never told any of the men I dated about my illness without a name, which doctors had been telling me was "all in my head."

My work, the pursuit of my license for private practice, and the demands of my health had become my new obsessions.

Thirty-six

The condo was becoming unlivable, with its stacks of accumulated newspapers that I lacked the strength to carry down four flights of stairs to the dumpster out back, the piles of laundry that had to be lugged down to the basement to wait their turn for the communal washers and dryers and then hauled back up again, and the refrigerator and cupboards that had become empty because I couldn't walk the length of the supermarket or carry the heavy grocery bags into the house.

At the post office, I saw a handwritten note: *Housecleaning, call Donna and Cathy.* When they came over to meet me and saw the mess I was living in, I think they felt sorry for me. With great kindness and generosity, they offered to do whatever housework I wanted, for however much I could afford, one morning every other week.

They made it possible for me to keep going. While I was at work they changed my sheets, did my laundry, took out my trash, and washed the floors, mirrors, and sliding door to the balcony with its fabulous view of the boat traffic in the canal.

———————

Getting groceries into the condo was still a problem, so I often ate out at a Chinese restaurant not far from the office. The food was good and also inexpensive, but I had to endure one hurdle before I could be seated. The young man from Shanghai who greeted me at the door always said, loud enough for everyone in the dining room to hear, "Just one?"

I hated that "just." Just one. I was just one. I was alone, and I did not appreciate attention—mine, his, or anyone else's—being called to that fact. I would have liked to request that he omit that word, but "four," "three," two," and "just one," seemed to be the only words of English that he, or anyone else working there, knew.

So I was just one. But I ate there anyway because there was no food at home, and I was too weak to shop and cook.

Cape Cod was an ideal place for couples, especially the many retirees who came down in pairs to play golf, dine in restaurants, and enjoy milder winters than they had endured inland. In the summer months that changed, as college kids poured in to work in the restaurants and shops that served the thousands of visitors who jammed the beaches until Labor Day, when all returned to normal, which is to say, quiet, elderly, and paired. When an elderly spouse died on the Cape, the one left behind often sought another lifestyle, somewhere else, because they were no longer part of the coupled world.

Carol drove down from Boston in January and suggested we go out to dinner at a restaurant that was open year round. I was in my late fifties, she about six years younger. After we were seated, she looked around the dining room filled with elderly couples. "My God, Sam," she said, "we're the youngest people here, probably the only people under eighty."

"That's the way it is here in the winter," I told her.

"How can you stand it!" she said, rather than asked.

All I could do was shrug. I had come to the Cape for a reason, to reconnect with my childhood memories, to walk the beaches and breathe the salt air, to heal, and find my life, my path, my future. Loneliness was simply the price.

Thirty-seven

My cousin Bob bought a condo on Plymouth Beach and we were neighbors. The six years difference in our ages had seemed huge when we were little, but now we could relate to each other as adults and get to know each other, walking the beach, lounging in beach chairs, talking about our memories and our new lives.

I also reconnected with an old college friend living on the Cape. Ruth invited me to join an exceptional group of women, some of them single, all of them professional, and united in their commitment to ethics, spirituality, and learning. They had named themselves The Outliers, the ones outside the normative curve. They were lively, intelligent, all about my age, of various backgrounds and religions, and I was finally among kindred souls. But the monthly meetings were potluck suppers, to which we were each expected to bring a dish. After the first few meetings I started giving excuses, not attending, pleading fatigue, which was real, but not telling them the larger reason was that I was too tired to cook or even shop for my share of the meal.

I realize now that I could have told them the truth and they would have offered me their food, their help and support, but something else was taking over my life, and it was my ever-present, deeply ingrained sense of shame. I was ashamed of my weakness, my constant fatigue, and my aching body, and I was putting all my limited energy into covering it up, not letting anyone see how much I struggled just to show up for work and make it back home. Every doctor I saw told me there was nothing wrong with me. If there was nothing medically wrong with me, then there seemed to be only two possibilities: either I was some kind of crazy person, unable to think my way through the normal activities of every day, or I was simply an inadequate human being. I couldn't let anyone know that after all these years, all this education, all my efforts, I was glaringly, indisputably, shamefully, simply, and totally inadequate. So I never let on that I was ill, in pain, and struggling to meet my basic needs for food and sleep. No one—not even Elias or Ruth or Bob—knew about that.

———————

I was having post-surgical issues requiring another operation, so I had surgery in Boston at the end of March and came home to the condo, only to be driven to the local hospital by my friend Nancy two weeks later, in the wee hours of the morning, with gangrene in my gall bladder. Medication I had been taking for pain had masked a growing infection, which was now raging out of control. After two days of intravenous antibiotics, I was operated on again, my fourth major surgery since Becca's death eight years earlier.

I returned to the condo only a few weeks before the date of my bat mitzvah. I told Elias and the women in the class that I didn't think I could be ready in time, and that they should proceed without me. I was bowing out.

"As if we would let you!" Elias retorted with a warm smile. The class began meeting at my condo so that I could participate.

One symptom of the sleep deprivation I had been experiencing for more than two years was loss of memory, and I was finding memorizing my Hebrew speaking part extremely difficult. I consulted my friend Martha, who was a gerontologist, because I figured that memory loss is a common problem among the elderly.

"Use a different learning tool," she advised. "If you're accustomed to learning visually, switch to auditorily. Or if you usually learn by reading, try writing. The point is to use a different part of your brain than you've been using."

So I drew musical staffs on a sheet of paper and wrote my part in musical notation, like a song, which fit the style of chanting that is used in Hebrew. Then I marked the words and phrases with colored highlighters, so that the intonations were yellow going up the short scale, and pink coming down, with blue on the final word of each phrase. I taped the finished piece to my bathroom mirror and "sang" my part when I combed my hair, brushed my teeth, put on or washed off my makeup, every morning and evening.

Nancy, also a member of the bat mitzvah class, helped me find a dress that concealed my now swollen belly, and assured me I looked fine. Donna and Cathy offered to set up and take down the buffet I would be providing for my guests at the reception following the service. And on May 11, 1996, at the age of fifty-eight, I was called to the *bima* (altar) as a bat mitzvah, a daughter of the Torah. My parents were present, and I wore my father's *tallith*, or prayer shawl. I realized with a shock how very old he had become when I saw from my place on the *bima* that when the congregation stood to honor the Torah, he remained seated. At almost ninety years old, he had become too weak to stand.

Despite the fact that he had not wanted to give me his *tallith*, that he had thought it "wrong" for a woman (my mother had insisted that he give it to me), he told me afterward that my Torah reading had been perfect. Especially coming from my father, this was high praise, and I finally felt fully validated by him.

Thirty-eight

Private practice of psychotherapy was still my goal. After a year and a half at the Federation, I left in search of work that was more clinical. I picked up part-time or temporary positions at a rehabilitation hospital, a hospice, a nursing home, and a clinic, and I still responded to on-call work at the hospice closer to Boston where I had trained. So I had more than enough opportunities to work. All I lacked was energy, and for that reason could work only limited part-time hours.

When I had a full day to put in, I'd go to the office in the morning and come home an hour later to nap on the couch. Then I'd go see a patient in their home or in the hospital and come back to the condo again to sleep. After another patient in the afternoon and another nap, I'd be back at the office at about seven p.m., completing my paperwork.

I pushed myself because I needed the income, but more than that I needed 3,500 hours of supervised work to qualify for my license to have a private practice of psychotherapy. For someone able to pursue the degree and the independent license full-time, the process took four years—two of full-time school, and two of full-time work following graduation. But with my need to work while attending school, and my exhaustion following school and cancer surgery, it was taking me more than twice as long. I was closing in on the required total, and at the rate I was going could look forward to completing the hourly requirement in one more year. I had to push on. I saw no other option.

I prayed a lot. I wrapped myself each morning in the *tallith* that my father had given me, covering even my head, signifying the beginning of my time for prayer. I read from *Daily Word*. Then I recited my own modified version of Jesus's prayer from his Sermon on the Mount, changing most of the words but keeping the sentiment and making it relevant to me. "Our Father, who art in heaven" became "Goodness and love which is everywhere." I might also read a psalm, and then write or meditate in silence. I needed to feel hope that I would get

160

well, that life would get easier, that I wouldn't always be lonely and sick and struggling. I needed a partner, and I chose as my helpmate the Great Mystery, because when I felt connected to the vast, universal forces of love and goodness, I felt stronger, optimistic, and more competent. I wasn't really alone.

When I finished my prayers, I folded the *tallith* and placed it back in its blue velvet bag, until the next day.

Aurora was a psychic, or not actually a psychic, but a reader of some sort who, I was told, was very gifted and worth the long trip and the fee to get a reading from her.

Over the phone, she asked for my birth data—date, time, place, name given to me at birth, and a few other details— and told me it would take her two months to interpret it all and have a report for me.

I saved my money and arrived at my appointment as instructed, with a tape recorder and two hours worth of blank audio tape. I still have the tapes, but have never felt the need to listen to them. What she said felt true, and stuck.

She told me that in my past lives (*I hadn't known we were going to talk about this!*) I had been a writer, but my writing was a craft rather than a creative art. I wrote what other people said. I was a scribe of sorts. But the purpose of this life, the life I'm living now, she said, was to use my skill with words, developed through many lives of earning my living by writing, to help others heal.

"By the way," she interrupted herself, "what do you do for work?"

I told her that I was a clinical social worker, doing psychotherapy for hospice patients and their families, and for people struggling with difficult life issues such as illness, relationships, fear, and sadness.

Her eyes widened in amazement. "You're doing exactly what you were meant to do," she said.

"I know," I responded. I had spent my whole life working toward this, struggling to interpret the signposts along the path to my Right Livelihood. I had known since I saw my first client, in my first internship six years earlier, that I was doing what I was born to do. Still, the validation felt good.

She told me much more, and then invited my questions.

My first one was, "Will I ever write a book?" I've always felt there was a book in me, needing to be born, but I wasn't sure yet what it was about.

161

She examined the notes in front of her. "Hmmm," she said, "well, you're meant to."

My next question was, "Will there ever be another love in my life, someone wonderful to live out my life with?"

She consulted her data and frowned. "Not until after your sixty-third birthday," she said.

"I don't want to wait that long," I pouted, half joking.

"Well, you're going to have to," she snapped, annoyed. "Because that's how long it's going to take. First, some other things have to happen."

She consulted her data more closely, to see what "other things" needed to happen first. "Before you can meet someone . . . " she caught her breath and stopped.

"I know," I said. "My parents have to die." They had already become more frail, needing more help with everything.

She was silent for a moment, then quickly changed the subject "Besides," she said, "that name you chose, 'Samantha White.' The numbers are all wrong, you'll never get together with anyone as long as you have that name."

"Oh!" This seemed important. "What do I have to do?"

She thought. "Give yourself a middle initial," she said. "Anything to break up those numbers. Pick a letter."

I cast about. "How about 'M'?" I offered.

She did some math on the corner of her page of data. "Perfect!" she declared.

"Do I need to go to court again to change it?" I asked.

"No," she said, "just start signing all your checks that way. Put it on your business cards. Whenever someone asks for your name, just include the 'M'."

M. My middle initial before I changed my first name to Samantha had been M. In court, when I finalized my new name, the judge had asked me, "Are you going to be fine without a middle name?" and I had said yes.

M. What would it stand for? *Middle name. Mystery name.* It didn't matter. I would henceforth be Samantha M. White, the Woman Who Listens and can *Meet* someone wonderful and fall in love for keeps.

———————

My body hurt all over now. Sleep was impossible and I was exhausted all the time. At work, I focused on my clients and patients, but at night, at home, lying on my bed in the dark, there was only me and the pain, and it pummeled me so that I couldn't think of anything else. I lay awake more aware of the soreness in my hips, shoulders, back, and legs than I was during the day.

The memory foam mattress with the foam egg-crate pad on top was no longer enough. After fitful dozing, if I was lucky enough to get even that, I arose each day more tired than I had been the day before. I felt sick, and very weak.

I tried alternative therapies—acupuncture, myofacial release, polarity, cranio-sacral and energy release—all of which cost money that I couldn't afford, but I was so desperate. I stayed with each therapy until it became clear it wasn't helping, and even the energy worker would shrug her shoulders and say, "I don't know what else to do."

I started going to a muscle therapist who did more than massage; she knew how to isolate and work with each muscle. No matter how gently she touched me, it hurt. One day I pointed to the spot that was hurting the most that day, and asked, "Marcia, what's the name of this bone?"

"That's not a bone, Sam," she said. "It's a muscle."

"But it's hard as a rock," I said. "It can't be a muscle."

She shrugged and looked at me sadly. My problems seemed to have to do with muscles that had become hard as bone, and hurt all the time.

I was sure that no one would hire or keep me on if they knew how sick and limited I was, so I put all my energies into maintaining the facade of a fully able, highly functioning woman, and fooled everyone. I performed well at work, walked bravely to my car at the end of each workday, drove home feeling the pain in my back and legs, made my tired, hurting way up the stairs to my rented condo, and collapsed on the couch, depleted, hungry, and in tears.

The next day, and every day, I did it again.

If I had a disease with a name, it would have served as the explanation for my limitations. But with all the doctors telling me there was nothing wrong with me, I had simply become a failure at daily living, less of a person than everyone else. I was more than ashamed—I was humiliated, embarrassed, and afraid that the tight community on Cape Cod, where gossip traveled fast, would discover my competence was only an illusion, and I was a fraud.

Part IV

Emerging

Thirty-nine

Someone told me about a group being run by a skilled facilitator who always led great programs. "It's free," she said, "and it will be wonderful."

It was called an Affinity Group, and I had no idea what it was, but I signed up anyway.

The format was tightly defined. Ten of us sat on chairs arranged in a circle, and each had a turn to speak for eight minutes. The rules were that when someone spoke, it had to be about personal issues, not the weather, sports, or politics, but about relationships and emotions. We were to give the speaker our full attention and not respond in any way—not then, not later, not ever. We met this way once a week for ten weeks.

I found the speaking part easy enough, but the listening was brutally challenging, because I wanted so much to respond. A beautiful young woman in the group talked about feeing ugly, and I wanted to tell her that she was mistaken, that she was gorgeous. A young man talked about how ashamed he was of being gay, an older man talked about wanting to leave his alcoholic wife, and I wanted to comfort and support them with words, but I had to just listen. I hated feeling muzzled.

By the third week, I noticed that my emotions were going through a change, and I was inexplicably angry much of the time. When my turn to speak came, I talked about this. Other people, when it was their turn, said that they, too, were feeling angry without knowing why.

As time went on, we all moved through emotions that seemed to evolve from despair to anger and then something else, something different for each of us. By the end of the ten weeks, everyone had taken some sort of action to begin to resolve the problem they had initially presented.

That was when I learned the great, positive value of listening, and of being heard, and realized that as a therapist, if I were to say nothing

167

at all to my clients during therapy, I would be helping them just by giving them my full attention and hearing what they were saying. If I had anything positive to add, it would be a bonus, but if I was in any doubt about the usefulness of what I wanted to say, I would do well to remain silent.

I sat between two friends at the temple's Sabbath service, feeling shaky, thinking of Becca and bracing myself to hear her name read. The date was her *yahrzeit*, the anniversary of her death, and her name would be read along with others who had died at that time of year. "If I could have cried, wailed, keened at her funeral," I had confided to Elias, "maybe I would be carrying less grief locked inside me. If only I could have let it out then! But I have never been able to, not once, since she died."

Elias began the sermon he had written with me in mind, as his gift to me. He spoke of the Holocaust, of pogroms in Russia, of centuries of war and genocide and tragedy, of all the victims of violence whose blood had been spilled on the earth, and in my vulnerable state I reacted to the image of the "blood-soaked soil" he spoke of, remembering Becca's death. My friends held me as I finally was able to collapse and sob uncontrollably, in public, for my lost daughter, the way I wished I had been able to do at her funeral.

Nine years had passed, and I still hadn't finished grieving.

In the spring I finally attained the required 3,500 hours of professional work under supervision, and was qualified to take the advanced-level licensing examination. I had been studying for the exam, taken a preparation course, and taken sample exams, which I had failed. I went to Connecticut for a weekend course, staying with my friend Laura, and the weekend had been a disaster. I arrived exhausted, dragged myself to class and back, and collapsed, with no energy to be with Laura. The course didn't seem to help, my brain couldn't take in the information and hold onto it.

On the advice of a friend on the staff at BU, I purchased some test preparation materials that came with telephone support. I studied, called for the available support, and took more sample exams. I failed them all.

I sought out my friend Martha, who had given me the brilliant coaching that had helped me learn my part for my bat mitzvah.

"Sam, just go take the exam. Don't tell anyone you're taking it, so you won't have to tell anyone you failed it. Maybe you'll pass it, but if you don't, it will still be good practice."

I registered for the next scheduled exam without telling anyone. The night before the test I prayed—to God, to Becca—"Please let the exam questions be ones I know the answers to."

On the day of the exam, I brought along some fruit and peanut butter crackers for energy, and a thermos of tea to help me stay awake. I arrived early and let the proctors know that I would need to take snack breaks. As I sat down with my pen and test materials and waited for the signal to open the exam booklet and begin, I looked around me.

Apparently the building had originally been a church. The walls were of slate and ornately carved. About twenty feet above the floor, wrapped around the room in a single line, were the words, "The Lord is my Shepherd; I shall not want. He maketh me to lie down in green pastures: He leadeth me beside the still waters. He restoreth my soul: He leadeth me in the paths of righteousness for His name's sake. Yea, though I walk through the valley of the shadow of death, I will fear no evil: for Thou art with me; Thy rod and thy staff they comfort me. Thou preparest a table before me in the presence of mine enemies: Thou anointest my head with oil; my cup runneth over. Surely goodness and mercy shall follow me all the days of my life: and I will dwell in the house of the Lord for ever."

It was the Twenty-third Psalm, in its entirety, above me and all around me. I was stunned. There was a message here—the same force that had held me up and pulled me through this far, still seemed to be with me.

I poured some tea from my thermos into its cup and accidentally spilled some on the table. *My cup runneth over,* I observed to myself with a smile, and at the signal to start I lit into the exam.

I checked the length of the test (170 questions) and divided the allotted time (four hours) by that number, and calculated the rate at which I would need to work to complete the test without rushing, allowing for three breaks. Then I studied each question carefully, considered all the possible answers, and answered with a measure of certainty that felt new to me. I stood up at my planned intervals to stretch, go downstairs, eat some crackers, and then resume the test.

When I had finished, with time remaining, I went over all my answers and decided to stand by each one. I gave my test to the proctor, who fed it into the computerized grader, and I waited. In about five minutes my score printed out.

I had passed with flying colors! I could scarcely believe it. "Congratulations," the proctor said as he smiled and handed me my certificate of a passing grade and the instructions for completing the application for my license, the highest license in my profession.

I was in no mood to go home to my empty condo. I drove in the opposite direction instead and showed up in my parents' kitchen at four p.m.

"What's happened?" they asked in unison.

"I just passed my LICSW exam," I said tentatively, not quite believing it yet and also afraid that if I let my excitement out, the walls of the house would crumble, like the Biblical city of Jericho when Joshua blew his horn.

But they were not shy about showing their excitement. We fell into a group hug and jumped up and down a little, and then my mother said, "Let's celebrate!" and my father said, "Let's go out to dinner!"

Which we did.

——— · ———

I took a walk on the beach with my friend Freddie, a little older than I and recently married to a wonderful man. "We've been talking about you," she said, "because we are so happy together, and we want you to have what we have. So we talked about what to tell you, and we agreed that if we had met any sooner, neither of us would have been ready for the relationship we have now. So our advice to you is this: When the time is right, it will happen."

As soon as I got into my car I wrote those words on a scrap of yellow paper I found. I carried it with me in my purse wherever I went, and from time to time read what she had said: *When the time is right, it will happen.*

It was my new mantra, my new prayer, and I believed in the truth of it.

——— · ———

People had been referring private clients to me whom I had been unable to accept before I had my license to practice independently, but now I could start accepting them. I had new business cards printed, and had fun choosing the ink color (teal) and a logo (a seashell). All I needed was office space. Sandy, who had been my clinical supervisor at the Federation, had an office with a group practice on the Cape that she would rent to me by the hour on the days she wasn't using it.

I started out with one client, referred to me by a minister. To maintain the appearance of being established, I arrived about fifteen minutes early to settle in. Two minutes before the appointment time, I walked to the waiting room, greeted my client, and ushered her in. When the appointment ended, I hastily wrote my clinical notes, placed an envelope containing the rental fee into the mailbox in the office, and left, after first checking that my client had already pulled out of the parking lot. I was a therapist in private practice, at last!

Eventually a second client was referred, and then a third, and for the rest of the year I continued to work three days a week at the clinic, pick up some on-call or consulting work when it was available, and use Sandy's office on the day she wasn't there. My private practice was a reality, and it was growing. Soon I would need an office of my own.

Forty

MAY 1998

Elias, my friend and now also my rabbi, said, "Sam, the temple has a discretionary fund to help members of the congregation who need it. Why don't you let me lend you some of it to set up an office?"

I felt it was for needier people than I, single mothers trying to feed their children, working families who needed a car. I didn't feel entitled to accept money intended for charity. I was supposed to be self-sufficient.

So I continued to rent Sandy's office by the hour, and work part-time at the clinic.

And Elias continued to urge me to use the temple's discretionary fund. "You'll pay it back, Sam," he said. "Over as much time as you want, with no interest. I don't understand why you won't take it."

I was hoping that somehow I would save enough money to do it on my own. I scanned the ads in the newspaper daily for an opportunity to share an office with someone, until one day I saw an ad for an office for rent that seemed too good to be true. I drove to the address given, even though it was evening and all businesses were closed, and peeked in the windows. The building was in historic Yarmouth Port, close to the most central exit on the mid-Cape highway. It was in the classic Cape Cod mode, two stories with white clapboard siding and a porch, and was surrounded by a small lawn in front and a large gravel parking lot in back. The other offices housed an accounting firm, a group practice of pediatric medicine, and a fund-raising organization for Cape charities. I stuck my business card into the decorative moulding on the door, and went home to leave a message on the owner's answering service.

I saw the office the following morning and it was perfect. My entrance would be directly from the parking lot, my door opening onto the porch, and there was a private waiting room, an inner office, and a rest room. The rent was unbelievably low, and no lease was required. Again, good fortune was falling directly into my lap.

Placing a deposit on the office and furnishing it was going to cost more money than I had. I suddenly realized that Elias had been offering me what I needed, and what he seemed to believe I deserved. I also realized that with my growing practice I would be able to repay the loan, even if only in increments spread out over time. I called him.

"How much do you need?" he asked.

I named a sum I thought might barely cover my needs, if I budgeted carefully.

"Would you like to pick it up today," he asked, "or shall I mail it to you? You'll probably get it tomorrow."

Shopping for furniture and accessories was fun. The carpeting throughout, in the waiting room, hallway, and inner office, was the color of sand, and the walls a light blue. I already had a small sofa, in blue and white checked canvas, that looked nautical and summery and was perfect for the therapy office. I decided to furnish the rest with porch furniture, which was inexpensive, and to decorate with a beach motif. Being on the Cape made it easy to find the things I had in mind. Wicker chairs with flowered blue cushions were for the waiting room, and on the walls I hung framed prints of Monet's lilies and color photographs of beaches and boats. My friend Janet gave me hundreds of seashells and rocks to add to my own collection, which I displayed in woven baskets in strategic places, to make the office feel homey, like someone's porch in summertime. I bought a second-hand desk chair in beige that matched the carpeting. I found a filing cabinet that fit perfectly inside the big closet, which I set up to serve as my supply room, with shelves for paper, envelopes, and books, all concealed by the sliding closet doors.

On May 3, 1998, a Sunday, I had a grand-opening party for my family and friends, to show them my new office and celebrate the occasion. My first clients at this location were scheduled to be seen the following day, and everything was in place. My parents were too infirm to travel, but told me to buy champagne as their treat, so that they could be with me "in spirits." My mother also suggested that I decorate the office with balloons, which hadn't occurred to me.

My relationship with my parents had greatly improved in the ten years leading to this event. They had seen my hard work, appreciated my accomplishments, and admired my grit. My father now found in me a colleague with whom he could talk shop. Lawyers and social workers deal with many of the same issues, and frequently collaborate on behalf of their clients. I sometimes called him at work with a legal question regarding a client sitting in my office.

A few weeks earlier, my mother had said, "You would have made a wonderful doctor," referring to my unfulfilled wish of forty years earlier.

"Thanks," I replied, "but I'm really happy doing what I do now, and have no regrets."

It was true. I was grateful for my parents' unlimited support of what I had recently accomplished, and I understood their love for me better than I ever had before. They had always loved me and parented in the way they believed right, but by now our relationship had shifted to one of mutual respect and I no longer resented them. Our new relationship provided the space in which I could discover that I loved them, too.

Although they couldn't be with me in person that day, we shared the joy.

———————

I tied six helium-filled balloons, pink, blue, red, yellow, green and orange, to the railing of the porch. The day was sunny and bright, and it was the anniversary of Becca's death. Getting from her death to this dedication of my work to her memory, to honor her goodness and carry on the compassion she had felt for others, had taken me exactly ten years, to the day. I decided that after the party, I would release the pink balloon and let it sail skyward, to her.

Nancy came, and Sandy, and Elias, and friends from various places on and off the Cape, and Sasha surprised me by showing up after having told me she would be unable to be there. Kathy, who had just opened her own law office, brought a white lily in a ceramic pot, and Marilyn and Mike sent a lush floor plant in a wicker basket. There were smaller plants for the window sills, and vases of flowers that people brought or had delivered.

I had put out cheese and crackers, fruit, coffee, pretty napkins and the champagne, which we used for a toast. We were all jubilant, and did a lot of posing for the camera—holding up our champagne glasses and grinning, arms around each other—and when I discovered that there was no film in the camera, we laughed. It didn't matter, the images of that day are burned into my memory, one of the loveliest

174

days of my life, when a dream came true, and I was surrounded by people who cared enough for me to share my joy.

I mentioned to my guests that it was the tenth anniversary of Becca's death, and that I planned to release the pink balloon to her, but several informed me that helium balloons pose a danger to birds, who mistake them for food and choke on them. So I abandoned the idea, albeit sadly.

After a couple of hours of celebration, we said our good-byes and everyone left. I stayed to put away the remaining snacks and ready the office for clients the next day.

I was sixty years old and warm with the glow of the love of the people who had helped me get to where I finally was, at my goal, doing the work that I most wanted to do. This—the office, the occasion, the brilliantly beautiful day, and my friends gathered to celebrate—was for Becca, to honor her memory for the rest of my working life by doing something positive, work that contributed in some small way to the greater good. It had cost me my home and my health. It had been worth it. I had reassembled the fragments of my shattered self, but now I was a different vase, more precious but less fragile, and more authentic. I was happier with the Samantha I had created using the pieces of who I had been before.

I finished tidying up. As I locked the door behind me, I noticed that one balloon was missing from the porch railing. Perhaps the wrapping of the string had been too loose to hold it in the face of the breeze coming off the ocean.

It was the pink balloon that was gone. The one I had wanted to release to Becca. I like to think that she had been there with us, celebrating, and before she left, took the balloon I had wanted her to have.

Forty-one

Fast-forward twelve years.

My day starts, as usual, with the chiming of the Zen clock in E-flat, a lingering, sonorous, single chime that taps into my consciousness, interrupting a dream. I ignore the chime, watch the dream recede, and start to wonder where I am. It was a pleasant, silly dream, as most of my dreams are these days. (Becca comes to me only occasionally, and those dreams can still upset me.) I waken slowly. My body hurts all over, and my skin is on fire. I remember what I must do. I focus on the pain, breathe, and patiently wait for the pain, the burning to go away. The clock chime sounds again, lingers, and fades. I am not yet ready to open my eyes, and I hurt too much to move.

I try to remember whether last night was bad or good. "Bad" means that I was still awake at three, curled up on the couch with Lacey (who stays at my side wherever I go and, although she is a white toy poodle, can out-snuggle and out-nap any cat), sipping lavender tea and watching reruns of old sitcoms, trying to relax so I can go back to bed and fall asleep. On a "good" night, all it takes for me to fall asleep are pain medicine late in the day and again at bedtime, a hot bath with aromatherapy, maybe an anesthetic patch on one hip or the other, and something very boring or silly to watch on TV, to dull my mind and make me laugh and relax.

Each day I monitor my symptoms in order to predict what I'll need at night. Sometimes I have several days in a row that are pain free, and other times a week of elevated symptoms. With my illness, the pendulum swings, the symptoms come and go.

I don't think I was up during the night, so it was a "good" night, and this is a good morning. The chime sounds again, still softly, but the interval between chimes is getting shorter. I feel Lacey curled up on the blanket behind my shoulder, leaning her full nine pounds into me. I open my eyes. I don't know how long it takes, two minutes or ten, it doesn't matter. I wait, and using the mindfulness meditation

176

that works for my chronic pain, feel the sharpness of it rise and then start to fall away.

Dave, my husband, has awakened before me, left the bed and opened the curtains, so that light pours in through the windows, helping me to wake up.

When I can move, I get up slowly and reach over to turn off the clock chime, then fall back onto my pillow. Dave has left the extension phone on his pillow beside mine. I reach for it, press the intercom button, and hear the phone ring in the dining room.

"Good morning," he croons, his voice gentle, loving, and warm.

"Hey, my handsome Drummer Man," I say. "How are you?"

"Great. Ready for your tea?"

"You bet," I say.

We hang up. I roll over and reach for the pillbox on my nightstand with its compartments labeled S-M-T-W-T-F-S, because I can never remember whether I've taken my pills. I prop up the pillows, drag myself to a sitting position, and am swallowing my first pills of the day as Dave opens the door and walks in, smiling, bringing me my favorite mug with jasmine green tea leaves steeping in the basket nestled inside, steam rising. He places the mug on the nightstand, and gives me the first kiss of the day.

"Mmmmmmmm," I say. "Thanks for the tea."

He smiles, kisses me again, leaves, and closes the bedroom door behind him.

God, I think, *how I do love that wonderful man!*

My fortune from the shrine at Nikko ("Don't travel in search of love. Stay home, and it will find you.") came true eighteen years after Paul and I had finally separated. During those years I had fulfilled many of my personal dreams of travel, romance, and career, and developed precious, lasting friendships. Along the way I learned to value myself and had finally become clear about what mattered to me in relationships—honesty, kindness, competence at something that mattered, and commitment. I met Dave on-line, where we connected over our shared love of jazz. He was like no one I had ever known before, and he all the qualities I was looking for, in abundance.

Before our first date I told him I have fibromyalgia. It was finally diagnosed in 2001, two years after I left the Cape for the mainland, to be closer to Boston's high-level medical care. He had never heard of it, so he looked it up on the Internet. After reading about it, he told me that he admired me for my fortitude in the face of my illness. I was ready to trust him with my heart.

Fibromyalgia is a syndrome, or a constellation of symptoms, including muscular pain throughout the body, insomnia, and all the complaints associated with sleep deprivation, such as chronic fatigue, irritable bowel, mental confusion, and memory loss. It is believed to be a maladaptive stress reaction, brought on by a tightening of the muscles in response to stress or trauma. The severe tightness causes all-over pain, which prevents sleep, resulting in more fatigue, and more stress, and the cycle goes on endlessly, even after the original stress and trauma have ended. I spent seven years going from doctor to doctor until I found Dr. Winchell, who recognized it in me and began my treatment, which is not a cure, but a way of controlling the symptoms.

Until Dave nursed me back to health I had been too tired to cook, and had been relying on packaged, processed foods, low in nutrition, high in chemical contaminants, for a long time. He learned how to cook healthy, delicious, organic foods, some of which—such as collards, daikon, and mustard greens—neither of us had ever eaten, took me to all the medical consults, saw me through three more surgeries, and helped me bring my symptoms under control. With his help I identified my food sensitivities and eliminated the culprits, and we embarked on a lifestyle based on healthy, balanced meals, gentle exercise, and adequate sleep. We make our health—mental, spiritual, and physical—a top priority. He has been all my prayers answered, all my wishes come true. He makes me laugh; he dances with me in the kitchen to the music on the radio; he showers me with his gentle love.

I smile remembering that my mother loved him when she met him, and had said, "Now I can die in peace, knowing you are not alone." Two weeks later she had the stroke that took her to a peaceful death. As life left her body, I held her in my arms and sang to her. She was ninety-three. My father, who died two years earlier, never got to meet Dave, but when both my parents had been healthier I had asked, "If after you die you find there's a heaven and you can intervene in my life, please find me a wonderful man and send him to me." I like to think that maybe my dad had seen into Dave's heart and mine, and known we would love each other and make each other happy.

For the next half hour I sip my tea, savoring the aroma of jasmine, letting the slight caffeine kick of the green tea help me waken. By the bright light of the lamp on the desk a few feet away, I read my inspirational passages for the day from the four books I keep on the headboard shelf: *Daily Word; Everyday Mind; Peace in Our Hearts, Peace in the World; and Buddha's Little Instruction Book*. Sometimes I add a page or two from Jack Kornfield's *The Path with Heart*, or I read one of Rumi's poems.

I pray.

When it comes to prayer, I am an equal opportunity supplicant. Sometimes I use the Buddhist form of metta prayer, addressing my gratitude and pleas to no one in particular, saying, "May I be peaceful. May I be happy. May I be well." I take it further when I ask, "May he find peace. May she be happy. May they be well." I also pray to the saints a lot, although I've never been a Roman Catholic, and it has worked. All my prayers have been answered and I have received many blessings.

I speak with God many times a day, but what I mean by "God" is not in keeping with any tradition I know of. It's my own concept of what is at work in the world, and "God" is, to me, a name, a perfectly good word, that I am willing to call it. Judaism uses a number of interchangeable words for the Divine, such as *Ha Shem*, *Adonai*, and *Ayn Sof* all of which only allude to the Nameless. I pray to the spark of Divinity, the fundamental goodness that I believe is in each of us.

I used to think that Paul owed me back the five years of care I had given him while he was ill. But I believe now that what we do goes out into the world and often comes back from a different direction. I gave Paul the gift of all I had, and then Dave found me in need and gave me the gifts of his love and care. As Grady taught me, *What goes around, comes around.* Buddhists call it Karma, theists call it God, agnostics credit the universe. What it is called doesn't matter to me. The forces for good have blessed me with much love, going out and coming in.

My first marriage lasted twenty-five years, and it has been longer than that since it ended. I am whole again, put together from the fragments of the shattered person I once was. I've grown in spirit, in faith, and in purpose, stronger than I was before, and more peaceful. I have created this new self of mine, different, authentic, my-self. Samantha. Happy now. I know that more pain and loss lie ahead, because that is how life goes, but I feel much better equipped to get through it and grow some more.

When I finish the tea and my morning prayer time, I feel ready to climb out of bed. "Come on, Lacey," I say, picking her up. Sometimes I carry her like a football against my side, relaxed, her legs dangling, other times like an infant, her eyes fixed on my face.

My first few steps are painful, my prosthetic hips protesting the movement and the burden of my weight and Lacey's combined. I know if I keep moving, the pain will usually go away, providing last night really was a good one, and I have slept long and deeply enough. If not, I'm facing a rough day of fatigue and pain, and I'll probably end up back in bed soon for the remainder of the day. That happens less and less, now that I have learned how to take care of myself and avoid stress—mental, emotional, physical—as much as possible. Stress of any kind, I've learned, exhausts me and makes me ill. That is probably how I developed fibromyalgia in the first place, by carrying too much stress in my heart, mind, and body.

Dave fixes breakfast while I check my messages and e-mails for any schedule changes. No emergencies, and no cancellations. I also notice no evidence in the living room of my having been up in the wee hours of the morning, no empty mug or box of crackers.

By the end of breakfast—oatmeal, rice milk, fruit, and my nutritional supplements—the pain is gone, I'm feeling fine and ready to face the day. I have three clients scheduled, all of them in the afternoon, and this evening I'll have dinner with Sasha. Rushing would exhaust me, so I'll need the remainder of the morning to slowly shower, dress, put on makeup, and get to my office in time for my first appointment.

If I had received the diagnosis of fibromyalgia sooner, and been able to receive good care before the damage to my body had taken such a toll, maybe I could have avoided being so physically compromised now, and would be able to bounce out of bed mornings and be in less pain. But I'm still one of the lucky fibromyalgia sufferers because I'm not more disabled, as many are. I have doctors who understand the illness, a treatment plan that works, and joy in living. I feel better now in my seventies than I did twenty years ago. I can walk, shop, work, keep up with the laundry, and stand in the kitchen—in ten-minute spurts—long enough to prepare an attractive, nourishing meal. I have learned how to take care of my body by eating right, sleeping enough, nurturing my spirit, and getting fresh air, natural light, and controlled exercise. I sometimes use a cane or a wheeled walker, depending on how much walking I need to do. Dave and I share the housework and play in a concert band together (I sit on a high stool at the marimba, while the rest of the percussion line stands), socialize with friends, and enjoy our combined families.

I'm grateful for my fibromyalgia diagnosis, for Dave, for our sheltering home, for my miraculous artificial hips, and for my rich and happy life, our families, and even for Paul, and Nick.

Becca had asked me once, "Mom, was it a mistake for you to marry Dad?"

As always, I answered her truthfully. "I haven't figured that out, Honey, but if it was, it's one I'm glad I made. Because if I hadn't married your dad, I wouldn't have you."

If I had made a mistake, maybe it was the mistake of thinking we could be happy together forever. Paul had given me all he had and two wonderful daughters, and when he needed to stop had pushed me out of my "safe place" and forced me to learn to become a complete person in my own right. Nick nursed my heart's wounds when I was hurting, fed me with the only kind of love he had to give when I was starving for it, and gave me the knowledge that I am lovable.

Given what I've experienced and survived, I know I'm lucky to be alive, in love, able to walk, and doing the work that fulfills my life's meaning.

I embrace it all, with gratitude.

Forty-two

POSTSCRIPT TO MY READER

The surprise for me in writing this book has been that in holding up my pain and grief to share with you, I uncovered an immense richness of joy that I had forgotten was buried underneath. As I dug through the memories of frustration, disappointment, loss, grief, trauma, and all the rest, happy memories began to bubble up through the new openings in the hardened crust of my old pain, and I began to remember good times I'd had, and nice things, loving things, that people had done for me, that had happened to me, that could define me as well as, if not better than, the pain I had started out to write about.

So the gift in writing this has been to myself as much as to you, in that by fully accepting my own painful story, and giving it the form of this book, my experience itself was transformed—from one of suffering to one of understanding, deep joy, and gratitude for the other parts of my life.

Everyone has their own mode of release, and sometimes we need to search for it. I believe that words, whether spoken or written, can be powerful tools for expression and release. I thank you for the gift of reading my words, in a sense being "someone to talk to" on my voyage of unearthing the happy memories I had lost.

I wish you a healed life of peace, purpose, and joy.

Samantha M. White

182

A Recipe For A Healed Life

MY RECIPE

The recipe I followed for my healing, when I felt broken and without much reason to live, has five main ingredients: Intention, Support, Meaning, a Goal, and Personalization. Each ingredient is explained in detail in the following short chapters. As with any recipe, this one can be customized and improved upon with more of one thing, less of another, and the addition of a surprise ingredient or two, to create a recipe that works for you.

The First Ingredient: Intention

First, we grieve.

Many models exist for how this happens, some of them overlapping, others unrelated, all of them helpful to consider, and none of them cast in stone. Grieving is an individual journey, and each person needs to find their own way through it. What all the models have in common is acceptance as the end result. Before we can move forward we must cry and rage and hurt and finally be able to say, "This has happened, and nothing and no one can change that." As the fence salesman at my kitchen table told me all those years ago, when we realized we had both lost children, the pain doesn't go away. Our task is to learn to live with it.

So my first step was the decision to learn to live with my emotional pain rather than to run away from it or waste my life waiting in vain for it to stop. I accepted that when I woke up each day I would find it waiting for me, and I would climb out of bed with it and bring it with me as I entered the morning, grateful for another day in which to heal—because I intended to heal, and knew from my study of techniques for creating one's own life (Chapter Eighteen), that it was possible.

Why did I bother? Because I couldn't bear to let all that anguish, loss, and sorrow go to waste. My pain became a giant resource, which could pollute my life and that of everyone I knew and loved, or I could transform it into something to be put to use, to make me stronger and more able to help others through their pain. When the pain is put to good use, it really doesn't hurt as much.

Is that disloyal to whomever we've lost? I believe it honors them, and speaks to our love for them. So intending to transform the pain into something that will have a positive effect in the world honors the suffering, the loss, the tragedy of what happened, and the people who suffered most.

I had to accept it all before I could move forward. Accepting the loss of someone dear, or of something longed for or treasured, does not mean not caring, not wishing it were otherwise, or feeling fine with it. It means being able to say, "I cannot change what has already happened, or control another person's actions." When we accept life just as it is, and then move forward courageously with that truth, peace can begin. Courage is not the absence of fear or pain, it is feeling the fear and sorrow and forging ahead anyway.

So we must grieve, for however long that takes, and allow that process to support our Intention to not only live with it, but to grow from it, to take us to healing-beyond-healing. We must accept that life has changed forever, and intend to make use of the experience, to not waste the pain but to grow from it.

That is the first ingredient of my Recipe: Intention to accept the pain and move forward in new ways. Without an Intention to heal, grief can last a lifetime, affording scant peace or purpose, and often precious little joy.

While working toward Intention, other ingredients of the Recipe can be explored and the steps begun, but grief, eventual acceptance, and Intention to grow from the experience, are the bedrock of any Recipe for the kind of healing that takes us beyond where we were before it happened.

The Second Ingredient: Support

The second ingredient, Support, the kind that comes from other people, can take many forms. I was lucky to already have loving, helpful people in my life when Becca died. But I needed more than they could provide, because some of them were grieving her death, too, and many who wanted to help me did not know how. Too soon, many drifted away, unable to continue to witness my suffering.

Talking to friends is a wonderful help in times of trouble, and I am forever grateful for those who were able to listen to me for so long. Family and friends, however, are personally invested in our happiness, and because they care about us may hope we will heal in a certain way or direction, or at a certain speed. For balance and a realistic perspective, bereavement groups (Bereaved Parents, Compassionate Friends, and so forth) and twelve-step programs (Al-Anon, Alcoholics Anonymous, Overeaters Anonymous, and so forth) provide effective Support, and so does professional help, carefully chosen. I favor working with a good psychotherapist, but a life coach or a spiritual leader of any faith or orientation also has much to offer. I sought the advice of, and read books by, everyone I could think of, including therapists, nurses and doctors, Buddhist teachers, energy healers, art teachers, nuns, ministers, priests, rabbis, shamans, gurus, a music therapist, and a psychic. Professionals bring their unique skills and perspectives to our problems, which nicely complement the loving point of view of those to whom we matter personally.

Meeting with a therapist was very different from turning to people I knew. Having someone to talk to, and cry to, who had no personal agenda and did not judge me, who was a skilled listener and understood how to do good therapy, was an essential part of my Support system.

Psychotherapy was invented long ago as a cure for mental illness, but it never lived up to the hope. However, until the advent of modern psychopharmaceuticals (medications for depression, anxiety, psychosis, and so forth), there was no effective alternative, so psychotherapy

189

remained the only, albeit ineffectual, option, and became thought of as treatment for "crazy people." Now we understand the biological nature of mental and behavioral disorders, and treat them with medications or alternative healing approaches such as nutrition, natural remedies, light therapy, music therapy, hypnosis, and many forms of energy balancing.

But while this medical approach was developing, psychotherapy showed itself to be a valuable tool for the mentally healthy as a technique for improving coping skills. That is what psychotherapy is now—a tool for assisting healthy people to identify and achieve goals related to improving the quality of life. For people suffering from behavioral, mental, or medical disorders, psychotherapy is a highly useful adjunct to medical or alternative treatment. For everyone, it's another approach to identifying and managing painful thoughts and emotions, breaking destructive habits, and choosing behavioral changes, to achieve greater satisfaction with life.

Whenever possible and safe, a good therapist leaves the decision-making and control of our lives in our hands, so that the solution is consistent with our own hopes and values. We need not weigh our words, concerned that personal revelations will shock or hurt the feelings of the therapist. The conversation is further protected by confidentiality, which the therapist should explain at the first meeting. Having a trusted, skilled listener in the room bolsters our courage to be honest, and provides safety and Support around the discovery of what has been buried inside us, afraid to come out. Our words can come up from deep within and we can hear and honor them, possibly for the first time.

The most valuable training I ever received for being a therapist was being a client. As both, I believe three elements are essential for successful therapy.

First, the therapist must be someone the client likes, feels comfortable with, and trusts. Psychologist Dr. Carl Rogers said that it is the relationship between client and therapist, itself, that heals. The therapy, then, can be only as good as the relationship. Not all therapy is the same and not all therapists work in the same way. If you have had a negative experience with therapy, you and the therapist may simply have been a poor fit. Find someone you respect and admire, from whom you feel respect and admiration coming back to you. Shopping around for therapist with whom you feel comfortable is a totally sound approach, and any therapist who objects to being interviewed (you, or your insurance, pay for that hour as you would any therapy session) would be suspect, in my opinion.

The second element for effective therapy is the client's willingness to change something about themselves if it is contributing to their unhappiness. The client is almost always the healthiest member of any dysfunctional group, family, or couple, the one who knows it isn't working right, but nonetheless must be willing to alter the dynamic, to be the force for change. The change may be the very thing the client most fears doing, but the therapist is there to help.

The third element of successful therapy is perseverance, hanging in long enough for the process to work. It takes time. The therapist in Chapter Four who told me to "come back when you're in enough pain" was not doing therapy. Good therapy meets the client where the client is, and gently accompanies the client to a point of willingness, understanding, and ability to find and accept a solution. I did ultimately divorce Paul, but I was in no way ready to do that when I first met that therapist—which is why I was seeking therapy! Years of good therapy, when I needed Support to help me come up with good solutions, eventually took me to a new, healthier place of thinking.

As we heal, we become increasingly able to help and support others. One of my clients, a very religious woman, told me she believed God had brought her to me.

I thanked her for the compliment and responded in language I knew was familiar to her, that of the Bible. "Did I ever tell you," I asked her, "about my T-shirt idea?"

"No," she said, furrowing her brow, "I don't think so."

"Well," I said, "do you know the Twenty-third Psalm?"

"Of course."

I saw her eyes glaze as she mentally ran through the familiar psalm of comfort, and I gave her time:

The Lord is my Shepherd; I shall not want.

He maketh me to lie down in green pastures: He leadeth me beside the still waters.

He restoreth my soul: He leadeth me in the paths of righteousness for His name's sake.

Yea, though I walk through the valley of the shadow of death, I will fear no evil: for Thou art with me;

Thy rod and thy staff they comfort me. . . .

191

"Well," I said, after her eyes told me that she had reached the end, "I have this idea for a T-shirt I'd like to wear. It would be a dark burnt-orange color, with a gray logo and lettering, so it would be difficult to read, sort of shrouded in fog. On the front would be a big, round logo that said, 'Valley of the Shadow,' and on the back, one word . . ."

She looked at me expectantly.

"Staff," I said.

She paused only a second before erupting into hearty laughter.

"I'm on the staff," I said. "I work for God in the Valley of the Shadow of Death, because having spent so much time here, it's familiar territory and I'm not afraid of it. In fact, I'm honored to have this job. So maybe you're right, and this is what God wants for you, to come through this bleak time in your life, arrive at feeling better and living more fully, and have someone like me to walk the way with you."

That's therapy as I see it, having someone as your guide to walk with you through the dark and dreadful times, the painful, difficult times, someone who knows the way from having walked it with others, or perhaps even walked it on their own personal journey. Having walked it many times, good therapists speak to your needs by their presence and attention. They say, "Don't worry; just walk. You're doing fine. You'll make it. Trust me. I'm with you."

The Third Ingredient: Meaning

My third Recipe ingredient, Meaning, could be any helpful, pragmatic, spiritual, or religious faith or view of life's purpose, and a practice to go with it. While this might be an organized church-or-temple-based religion, it needn't be. Someone who has a religion or spiritual belief can turn to it in times of pain and sorrow, draw strength and guidance, seek spiritual direction, and pray. But for those who for any reason have not connected to a spiritual path, there is more work to do.

Not being committed to any one religion, I needed to find my own Meaning in life, and over time, I did. By thinking this through very deeply, and seeking spiritual strength and courage everywhere I could, I have come to feel comfortable in the houses of worship, and draw strength from writings, of many faiths. I've done this by finding what I can accept, and defining it in a way I can believe.

One of the biggest obstacles to finding comfort in religion, for atheists or people who have rejected the religion of their upbringing and the concepts they were taught as children, or who resist the language of the church, are what I call the loaded words—loaded in the sense of being laden with sacred Meaning for those who believe in them, and charged with negative connotations for those who don't. God is such a word, and so are Father, Lord, heaven, kingdom of heaven, Christ, Savior, etc. Words like these, unquestionably holy to many, can bring other seekers, previously disenchanted or somehow alienated, to a screeching halt.

This is because some of us have been taught to attach images to the words, images which may not be consistent with their spiritual meanings and are subject to interpretation. I was taught that God was a superhuman male being who lived in the sky, which was called heaven, but the time came when I could no longer believe that. I also thought that Jesus Christ was a rival God. But looking into the original meaning of the words and names has, for me, stripped them of the prickles that initially made me want to turn away. Rabbi Lieberman points out that in Jewish mysticism, God is sometimes referred to in ways that suggest God is, ultimately, unknowable and unnameable. Yet people have always tried to name the Divine, and describe it in human terms, because naming it that way makes it easier to think about, talk about, teach, believe in, and work with.

I believe that God can be what we need the name to mean. For me, God is the spark of love in each of us, taken collectively, and connected to each other like a net cast over the world. (I was delighted to find a Buddhist concept like this in the legend of Indra's net.) For me, the spark is always there, and God is everywhere, because goodness and love are everywhere, although there are people who are closed off to that part of themselves. Ironically, some people hate and hurt and kill in the name of God, but that's not my God. My God is peace and love. I can pray to God because I have identified it as goodness—in me, in you, and in everyone who is aware of their potential to contribute to the good of themselves and others.

Becca as a teenager asked me, "Mom, is God male or female?"

"Good question," I said. "What do you think?"

"I've decided that God can be either," she said. "Sometimes male, sometimes female. It's whatever we need God to be."

Smart girl! I thought, and said, "I think you're right."

When I recite what was taught to me in grade school as *The Lord's Prayer*, I feel free to use my own words, to evoke the spirit of what I believe. "Thy Kingdom come" may become "May love and goodness rain upon us." "Forgive us our trespasses as we forgive those who trespass against us" can be, simply, "May I forgive, and be forgiven." I can reframe the prayer to express my wish for support in being the best person I can be, keeping with what I believe is its meaning. There is lots of tradition for this, since prayers and psalms and the Bible itself have been translated into hundreds of languages, and interpreted in ever-changing ways, for thousands of years. If you don't know any prayers that feel acceptable to you, compose your own, which are about what you want and need to express.

The form of prayer addressed to no one in particular, as in "May I be healthy, may I be forgiving," is customary in Buddhism, which does not recognize a deity, and works very well for those who prefer not to use the word *God* (capitalized in this book out of respect for those to whom the word or name is, in itself, sacred).

Many people think that *Christ* is the surname of a man named Jesus. It is not a name, it is actually a word meaning "the anointed one," or one who is dedicated to God. I choose to understand it as the sacred, or Divine. Although it is a word I never use in my own thoughts and speech, when I encounter it in my reading or listening to others I take it to refer to the part of each of us that is sacred, our inner spark of Divinity. That way I can get past the misconception of it referring by name to the God of a faith that is not mine. "The Christ in each of us" becomes, to me, "the sacred spark we each contain (whether or not we choose to make use of it)."

———— ———

Since what I mean by "God" is difficult to explain, I sometimes use a different metaphor, one in which God is a worldwide corporation in which we each have a job description, and we can show up for work, or not. The job is always there. To show up for the *right* work can require some degree of soul searching. Some people know from childhood that they want to grow up to be a teacher or a doctor, others find themselves in their right job by circumstances, not even realizing it. Before I could find my right work, I had to consult a vocational counselor, go back to school, and train for seven years. But I'm sure I was always on the right path, because all my life experience supports what I do now.

This is an example of my God in action:

I was running late one morning to get to my job at a clinic on the Cape, and I didn't have time for breakfast. I had a full day of hour-long therapy appointments scheduled, with women who had been sexually abused and were being treated for trauma. They were disadvantaged women, some of them abandoned by their husbands, all of them with young children to care for, and their weekly meetings with me meant a lot to them. Those appointments meant a lot to me, too, and I wanted to give my clients the best attention I could. But I don't function well without breakfast, and to show up for work hungry and with low blood sugar would rob my clients of what they needed from me that day.

I ducked into the Dunkin' Donuts I passed on my way to the office for some orange juice, a muffin, and a cup of coffee to consume on the way. My heart sank when I saw a line of at least fifteen people stalled in front of what was apparently the only open register. This was going to take much more time than I could spare.

I turned to leave when a woman in a pink waitress uniform emerged from the back room, took in the scene, and called to me, "Miss! Step right over here!"

I looked at the long line of people ahead of me but she waved me over. "This register should be open," she said. "You shouldn't have to wait back there. Tell me what you need, it will only take a second, and then I'll wait on the others."

In less than two minutes I was out of there with juice, coffee, and a muffin, and she had waved my cash away. "Takes too much time to ring up," she said. "I apologize for the wait." She looked behind me. "I'll take the next person in line!" she called out.

I was struck by the weight of her kindness, which she will never know or imagine (unless she reads this and remembers). Because she had been kind to me, I was able to serve my clients that morning, and give them the best of myself. In turn, I hope each of them was able to be the best mother she could be that day, and progress a little further in her own healing.

That woman who gave me breakfast was working for the same corporation as I am, the one I call God, and we were working together, although she probably didn't know it.

So that's what I mean when I say that I work for God. I believe that we all can, that every life contains the potential for contributing to the greater good of all, even the lives of those who are sick or feeble and need to be helped, because they provide the opportunity for others to carry out their job description.

The woman in the donut shop called upon her spark of Divinity that morning, expressed as kindness. I treasure the feeling of connection I have with all the people who let that spark of goodness shine out from within them, because we help and hold each other up, and together we just might be able to spread love, joy, and healing where it's needed.

My spiritual practice, consistent with my beliefs, now consists of relevant reading (including *Daily Word*, Buddhist writings, and personal stories of triumph, which inspire me), meditating, working, and praying—and yes, I pray to God. Because words are the tools I love best, putting my pleas and my thanks and my affirmations in the form of words is probably why prayer helps me so much. Some people pray by creating art, others by making bread, cleaning house, singing, fighting fires, doing volunteer work—the list is endless. Anything that instills life with Meaning and purpose qualifies as prayer.

What you come to believe in, what gives Meaning to your life, may take time to develop. That's fine. Just start. Read inspiring literature, poetry and psalms; attend religious or philosophical gatherings, talk with kind and loving people, and find your own Meaning in your own life. Maybe for you it will be God, and maybe it will be something else—Nature, history, science. Just don't give up looking for the comfort that comes from finding Meaning in your experience or, more likely, imbuing your experience with Meaning.

The Fourth Ingredient: A Goal

The fourth ingredient in my Recipe is a personal Goal. Creating and organizing Mothers Against Drunk Driving was the personal Goal of Candice Lightner after her son was killed. Rabbi Harold Kushner, following the death of his son, wrote the book *When Bad Things Happen to Good People*. Foundations, memorials, legislation, and books have been created in response to painful loss, and even more people have dedicated themselves to more private Goals—distributing quilts, books, food, or furniture to the needy, achieving an educational landmark, providing transportation to the elderly—that list, too, is endless.

A personal Goal was essential for me. My Goal for my own healing was to realize my ambition to become a psychotherapist in private practice. I thought my clinical specialties would be bereavement and trauma, and while my practice started out that way, over time it has grown to include a surprisingly greater number of clients with bipolar disorder, so I have learned a lot about that condition, too.

I find that bipolar disorder and fibromyalgia have much in common. Both are chronic, and don't go away, but can be managed; both are strongly affected by the connection between mind and body, and can be treated; both are "silent," that is, they do not necessarily make themselves known to the observer; the person with either condition who commits to a treatment plan of healthy living, stress management, and medication when necessary, is indistinguishable from the person who doesn't have either malady.

Still, both are the kind of thing one doesn't want to mention in a job interview, because people fear you will have an "episode" on the job that will interfere with work. One of my Goals now is to help people understand these widespread conditions, respect the need for treatment, and lose the needless stigmas attached to them.

Psychotherapy can help greatly in managing stress, monitoring symptoms, and creating and following a plan of care.

Figuring out what I wanted to do, and accomplishing it, took ten years, every one of them worth the effort and expense, and although it couldn't bring back what I had lost, reaching my Goal gave Meaning to all of it.

———————

Your personal Goal can be anything you want or need it to be. Start small, or aim high. If you have already accomplished your Goal, design a new one. Here is where a good therapist or life coach or spiritual director can help you sort out your thoughts and choose something that aligns with your values. Make it about something you love, or would love, to do. Give it time; don't give up; and keep moving in the direction of your choosing.

The Fifth Ingredient: Personalization

Like any recipe, this one can—and should—be adjusted to meet the needs of the individual. While grieving and healing are universal experiences, our paths through them are personal. You may find you need or want to make changes or add an extra ingredient or two, as I did. For me, it was making amends to people I had hurt, and thanking others.

As I was writing this book, I recalled ways I had behaved when I was grieving that offended some of my most treasured friends, who had pulled away from me. I had been angry and hurt, and blamed them for not understanding. When I realized the role that I had played, I needed to round out my Recipe with two more ingredients: Atonement (or making amends) and Giving Thanks. I apologized to those I knew I had hurt, and thanked those who had given me Support.

The letter I sent to my women's group read:

It has taken until recently for me to heal to the point where I could look back and see that I did a lot to alienate some of you. To all of you who were on the receiving end of my crazy behavior during those years, I apologize. I realize now that I was quite out of my mind following Becca's death, and had been building up to it for several years. I fell apart, was drained, and the only energy I seemed to have was anger. My anger may have helped me survive and move forward. I'm sorry that it hurt some of you.

To my friend Steve, whom I hadn't heard from in years, I wrote:

I have not forgotten, nor can I imagine myself ever forgetting, how present you were for me, and how supportive and helpful, during one of the most difficult parts of my life—Paul's relentless depression, the end of my marriage, Nick's betrayal, Becca's death. I remember that you and I talked almost daily throughout that long stretch, and I leaned on you, relied on you, and you were fully there for me. Thank you, from the bottom of my heart.

Those letters reconnected me with two of my dearest friends, but moreover gave me peace and a feeling of having owned up to my responsibility for my behavior. Guilt no longer gnaws at me.

200

Closing Notes

Summed up, the steps of my Recipe are:

1. Grieve completely, to arrive at acceptance and Intention to heal and grow.

2. Gather all the helpful people and resources you can, to establish your Support system.

3. Look for Meaning, something to believe in, and practice your beliefs with a daily ritual, prayer, or reading.

4. Choose something to accomplish, your individual Goal, and aim for it.

5. Personalize your plan.

I still use these five ingredients in my life. I remain committed to my original Intention of using what I learned from the pain of Becca's death for the healing of others. For my Support, I keep my family and friends close, and have a therapist to talk to when I feel the need for his particular skills and wisdom. I find Meaning in daily prayer and a practice of engaged Buddhism, which involves bringing the precepts of Buddhism into my daily life. I also always have a Goal in my sights, whether to write and publish a book, or to learn to play in a band, or to do the work I love best—meeting with my clients. I am quick to apologize and to thank. My life is rewarding, and I am grateful to be blessed with love, understanding, peace, purpose, and joy.

Whatever ingredients your Recipe contains, the key is to have a plan in mind, a path to start out on, and gentle hands to steady and support you. What you need to do will occur to you, and you will recognize it and follow through. You may need to read something in particular, or write a poem or a song, or take a long trip to new vistas, to clear your mind and your soul. Think each action through carefully, don't be impetuous, proceed slowly and steadily, and believe your intuition, the wise part of yourself that speaks silently from within you. There will be days when you feel you've lost ground, but if you keep your eye on the long path out of darkness you will see that you have made progress from where you once were.

"What about Hope?" you may be asking. "Am I supposed to give it up?"

No, but often we need to change what we hope for. Decide what is possible, and hope with faith in your heart that it will happen. My Becca will never come up my front walk, or call me, and say, "Hi, Mom!" But I feel her presence in my life, because she is a part of me. Because of my faith, I believe she is at peace. That is my hope, and I draw comfort from it.

———————

Believe in miracles! They happen, but we need to be ready and open to noticing and receiving them. Sometimes they are small, and arrive slowly and quietly. Be grateful for all that you can. End each day naming what you have accomplished, no matter how small, and the things for which you are grateful. The good things in life deserve to be acknowledged, too. Take the time to develop your plan; remind yourself of it every day; and take one day at a time.

May the days, over time, take you to the life you want.

Works Cited

Daily Word, November/December 2010, 33. Available online at http://www.dailyword.com

DeCarlo, Gary; Leka, Paul; Frashuer, Dale, *Na Na Hey Hey Kiss Him Goodbye.* New York: Mercury Records, 1969.

Eliot, T. S. "Little Gidding," *Four Quartets.* New York: Mariner Books, 1968.

Fishel, Ruth. *Peace in our Hearts, Peace in the World.* New York: Sterling Publishing, 2008.

Fritz, Robert, *Path of Least Resistance: Learning to Become the Creative Force in Your Own Life.* Ballantine Books, 1989.

Kornfield, Jack. *A Path with Heart: A Guide Through the Perils and Promises of Spiritual Life.* New York: Bantam Books, 1993.
————. *Buddha's Little Instruction Book.* New York: Bantam Books, 1994.

Kübler-Ross, Elisabeth. *On Death and Dying.* New York: Scribner, 1969.

Kushner, Harold S. *When Bad Things Happen to Good People.* New York: Schocken Books, 1981.

Luhan, Mabel Dodge. *Edge of Taos Desert: An Escape to Reality.* Albuquerque: University of New Mexico Press, 1987.

Smith, Jean Ed. *Everyday Mind: 366 Reflections on the Buddhist Path.* New York: Riverhead Books, 1997.

Stearns, Ann Kaiser. *Coming Back: Rebuilding Lives After Crisis and Loss.* New York: Ballantine Books, 1988.

The Holy Bible, King James Version. Wheaton: Tyndale House, 1976.

Samantha M. White, MSW, LICSW, is a psychotherapist and life coach in private practice. She has earned college degrees in Pre-Med, Chemistry, Computer Science, and Social Work, achieving her most recent degree, the MSW, at the age of fifty-five. Her career has spanned the fields of medical research, education, health care administration, business, and medical, hospice, and clinical social work, and she is a writer, educator, and public speaker. Although she has enjoyed worldwide travel, she has always been drawn back to her native New England by its glorious variety of seasons, winding roads, hilly terrain, and ocean beaches and bays. She lives in Massachusetts with her jazz musician husband, and for relaxation plays marimba and folk harp, and enjoys kayaking on local rivers and ponds. She can be reached through her website, www.samanthawhite.com.

259992BV00001B/57/P